ear--Daily Paper, One Year $16, Six Months $10, Three Months $5.

ANUARY 1, 1852.

{ L. PICKERING, G. K. FITCH, J. E. LAWRENCE,
EDITORS.

VIEW OF THE LEVEE, SACRAMENTO CITY, CALIFORNIA.

The accompanying engraving gives a very correct representation of that portion of Sacramento which lies along the bank of the river. The view was taken when the water was at a high stage, and it will be seen that steamboats and other shipping, are considerably higher than the buildings on the opposite side of Front street, as the wide avenue between the buildings and river is called. The levee, which is raised along the bank of the river, about four feet high, being wide enough on the top for a wagon road, is distinctly marked. Before the construction of this embankment, in February, 1850, the memorable freshet took place, which inundated the town, and for a time jeopardized its permanency. During the subsequent season, the Levee was built, at an expense to our citizens of over $200,000; since which time Sacramento has been in no more danger of an overflow than the city of New Orleans. The shipping lies below and above the city, and could not be embraced in the present view. Our space will admit a very brief enumeration of facts concerning this great inland mart of California. Sacramento City stands in about 38° 35', North Latitude, and 121° 21', West Longitude. It is about sixty miles above the mouth of the river Sacramento, and one hundred and twenty-five miles from San Francisco. The city plat was surveyed and laid off in January, 1849. The streets run at right angles, and are all eighty feet wide, except M street, which is the centre of the town plat, and one hundred feet in width. The first building was erected in January, 1849, which is still standing, being now three years old. Three or four other buildings were erected between that time and the last of the same year, the latter period being about the commencement of the magic growth of the city. On the 18th day of March, 1850, Sacramento City was duly incorporated by an Act of the Legislature. The first election under the new charter, was held on the first of April, 1850. In October, 1849, the population was about 2,000. In December, same year, it had increased to 3,500. The census of 1850 put the population at 7,000 permanent residents, and 3,000 transient people. We have no means of correctly estimating the present population. A new census of the State of California is provided for by an Act of the Legislature, to be taken during the present year. The present value of all the real estate in Sacramento City, according to the last assessment, is $3,763,970; personal property, $2,071,938; making a total of $5,835,808. Taxes collected during the present fiscal year, will be as follows : On real estate, $75,000; license tax, $60,000; harbor dues, $50,000; making the entire available revenue of the city $185,000. This estimate was furnished by the City Clerk, and is exclusive of all delinquences. The present indebtedness of the city is in the neighborhood of $400,000. The legitimate expenses of the municipal government does not exceed $80,000 per annum. During the continuance of the funding ordinance the expenses of government are limited to $100,000 per annum; the balance of the revenues of the city are set aside for paying off the public debt. Of the present citizens of Sacramento, many have succeeded in amassing considerable wealth, though property is distributed more equally among the mass,

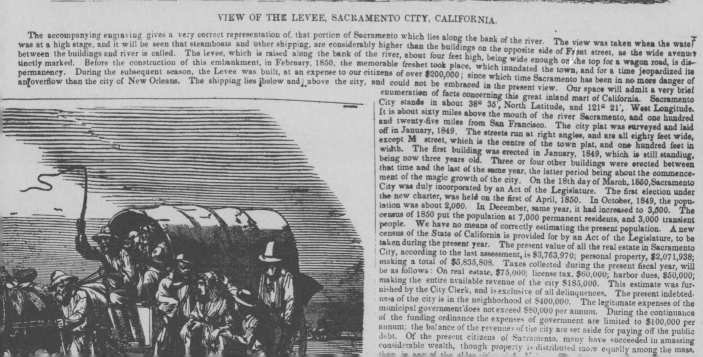

Sacramento

An Illustrated History
1839 to 1874

SACRAMENTO

An Illustrated History: 1839 to 1874
From Sutter's Fort to Capital City

by Thor Severson

California Historical Society

ACKNOWLEDGMENTS

Many contributed to the production of this book.

Allan Ottley, both friend and successor to Caroline Wenzel as chief of the California Section of the State Library, was good enough to read the manuscript and captions for historical accuracy.

Charles Duncan was responsible for research on text and pictures and contributed much to the manuscript.

William C. Glackin, critic in music, art, and theater, wrote Chapter Seven on the arts in early Sacramento.

Others who made significant contributions include Paul Johnson, John Beyer, Charles Jones, and James Henley.

Those institutions which made available collections for research and reproduction as well as personnel for consultation include, in alphabetical order: The Bancroft Library, University of California at Berkeley; Boston Museum; Library of the California Historical Society; California State Archives; California State Library; E. B. Crocker Art Gallery; M. H. de Young Museum; Henry E. Huntington Library; Oakland Museum; Sacramento *Bee* Printing Museum; Sacramento City-County Library; Sacramento City-County Museum; Society of California Pioneers; and Southwest Museum.

In Memoriam
CAROLINE WENZEL: HER BOOK

Following the death of Caroline Wenzel, for so many years chief of the California Section of the State Library, the California Historical Society appointed a committee to consider and decide upon a memorial that would suitably honor her memory. The committee discussed and researched various projects. Its ultimate decision was to try to translate into reality that which seemed to be the essence of Caroline's life: her love and devotion to books—especially those books or writings which dealt with the history and background of early California. The decision of the committee agreed upon, it then was approved by the Historical Society so that the chosen book, when ready for printing, would be offered to the Publications Committee as the first book in memory of Caroline.

From its inception, the Caroline Wenzel Committee has been a most congenial group, all ardent admirers of Caroline who singly and together were devoted to the one aim: to find the appropriate inaugural volume to be published in her name. Miners' diaries, Spanish manuscripts, voyages around the Horn, across the Plains: each was considered in its turn. But complete approbation never ensued. Something always seemed to be missing. Then one day in a meeting the remark was made: "It must be a book Caroline herself would want." That observation became the key to the decision. We all started looking back on our personal talks with Caroline. This probing carried me back to a day in the California Room of our State Library where Caroline occasionally would introduce me to writers whose research in Californiana she believed would interest me. That particular day she presented George MacMinn who was working on his *Theater of the Golden Era.* After Mr. MacMinn left, Caroline remarked his should be a very good and useful book. Then looking off wistfully, she added, "But of all the writers who come here for research I do wish one would produce my book." Asked what her book might be, she answered: "A book of prints of Sacramento with appropriate text."

When this conversation was relayed to the committee, someone said, "Caroline has described her own book. So be it." A distinguished and dedicated researcher devoted to all Californiana, Caroline Wenzel was deeply in love with Sacramento, her native city.

The members of the Caroline Wenzel Memorial Book Fund Committee —Michael Harrison, vice chairman, Warren Howell, Robert Power and Mrs. William Ely Chambers, now deceased—have met and worked together on this project over a long period of time. All agreed at the outset that the book chosen for production in Caroline's name must begin with the most careful research, aiming always toward Caroline's high standards. We only hope we have landed not too far off her star.

Dedicated to Caroline's memory on this day, the 15th of October, 1973.

ELEANOR McCLATCHY *Chairman*

Foreword

The determination was made early in the preparation of this book that the telling of the Sacramento story should begin at the beginning with the early Indian inhabitants of this fertile land, and should proceed through the rise and fall of John Sutter, the settlement brought by the Gold Rush, and the completion of the State Capitol in the early 1870s. It should be a chronicle, it was decided early, of the men who built the city, their time, and their test by flood, fire, and pestilence; of their beginnings in art, music, and theater; and of the establishment here of the Western terminus of both the Pony Express and the railroad which would link the Pacific and the Atlantic and bind the nation, seaboard to seaboard.

There is no conclusion to the Sacramento story, of course. There is only a pause to take stock, through narrative, of what was done. The reality is, the story of the building of Sacramento continues even as this book ends.

Contents

PART ONE

Foundations of a City

Young Sacramento City posed along the east bank
of the Sacramento River in 1849 for a sketch by
George Holbrook Baker. In 1885 Baker commissioned
George Frost to render the sketch in this impressive oil painting.
Both men became well known, Baker as a
printer-lithographer, Frost as a painter.

Introduction

Here was born the City of Sacramento,
   the City of the Plain, by the banks of two great rivers
   where they flow together in sensuous consummation.
In its infancy, outpost.
Then mining town, though miles from the diggings.
And port, though miles distant from the sea.
And when men turned from the mines, and back to sanity
and to things they could understand,
   they would build a new empire upon the lands of
John Augustus Sutter, and it would become queen city
   of a great and abundant valley,
   rich in agriculture and in trade;
   center of government and of a new adventure;
   and of a wealth far richer than the Argonaut dream.

Here rose the city, Sacramento.
   Here, a new life on the plain.
   Here, the wilds turned back,
   and empires built,
   and history made,
   not soon to be forgot.

The fort Sutter built took on this idyllic look by 1846. The illustration is from George H. Baker's *City of the Plain*, published in 1857.

John Augustus Sutter brought the first immigrants into the Sacramento area only to have his empire overrun and ruined by the Gold Rush. This W. S. Jewett portrait shows him in a dignified pose which is a combination of the military and nobility.

Sacramento City, 1849

Perhaps the most celebrated view of Sacramento ever made is that of George V. Cooper dated December 20, 1849. The expansive scene indicates a rapid growth of the city since Baker's sketch of mid-year. The large trees are still evident and the problems of putting a city on the muddy banks of a great river are indicated by the ruts in the street and by a huge hole in the center of J Street. The cavity is thought by some to have been caused by the removal of a tree.

The social center of early Sacramento City is highlighted at left in this detail from the Cooper lithograph.

The capstone of the cultural edifice was the Eagle Theater, center, which offered California's first professional theater and was combined with a flourishing gambling operation.

The city could not grow fast enough in spite of a phenomenal expansion. Business activity on the waterfront itself rivaled that of the formal city behind it. Auctions, impromptu restaurants, and commercial enterprises of many varieties set up shop under the trees or the temporary shelter of canvas.

Cooper's view of Sacramento City was the basis of countless similar pictures issued from all points of the world. A French version is shown above, and three other variations below. Though the artist himself made variations, some changes are clearly not his. Whether coincidence or plagiarism, it seems that in most cases Cooper was the only one of the artists who ever actually saw Sacramento City.

The Great Flood: 1850

For years before the January 1850 flood, Indians knew the banks of the rivers were periodically awash in certain places. But this flood was something else, something more sudden, and now, with the growing town beside the river, more serious.

Heavy December rains soaked the land, and on top of that the American and Sacramento both crested in walls of water. It happened so fast that flight was next to impossible for many and safe places were too far away. Some left in the first few minutes of warning, fleeing to the higher ground to the east.

Goods piled on the Embarcadero were simply swept away and other property losses were in many cases just as total. The lesson had been learned; there was no illusion of safety left.

By January 18, though, the rain was over for the moment, and the city had baled and dug and dried itself out. Rebuilding began and by February trading had already started again with the mines.

But the rest was a short one. Hardin Bigelow, later to be elected Sacramento's first mayor for his efforts, drove the townsmen in the construction of essential levees and dams for protection. Had he not, a new overflow in March would have had the same disastrous results.

Once the flood had hit in its full force and it was obvious that there was no way to keep the waters from running their course, the problem became one of survival and rescue.

Many died where they stood or slept, others perished of exposure floating on beds, crates, and bits of flotsam that would hold them.

The stories, rumors, and tales of those days and nights speak of heroes, fools, and knaves. One man is said to have gone down with his gold rather than give it up. Boats of any kind were hired and bought for grand sums and stolen with the fierceness of survival. Tents, boards, and canvasses were put up on any piece of high ground and jealously occupied.

The lithograph and details from it by Casselear and Bainbridge show the dramatic story of the first of many tests by the elements which the infant town was to survive. The finest hotels, the first theater, many businesses and homes were to be destroyed only to rise again with that curious determination of people set on staying where they are in spite of heavy losses.

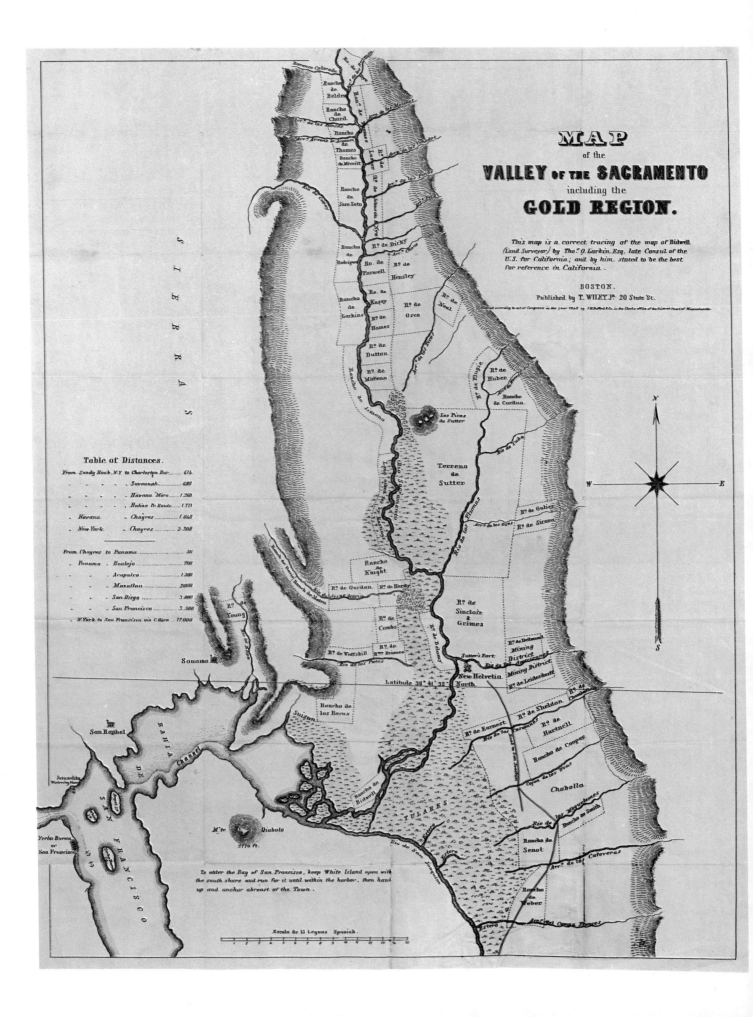

MAP
of the
VALLEY OF THE SACRAMENTO
including the
GOLD REGION.

This map is a correct tracing of the map of Bidwell (Land Surveyor) by Tho.º O. Larkin Esq. late Consul of the U.S. for California; and by him stated to be the best for reference in California.

BOSTON.
Published by T. WILEY Jr. 20 State St.

Table of Distances.

From Sandy Hook N.Y. to Charleston Bar	614
— — — Savannah	680
— — — Havana Moro	1.260
— — — Balize Br. Route	1.771
Havana — Chagres	1.048
New York — Chagres	2.308

From Chagres to Panama	50
Panama — Realejo	700
— — Acapulco	1.500
— — Mazatlan	2000
— — San Diego	3.000
— — San Francisco	3.500
N.York to San Francisco via C.Horn	17.000

Escala de 15 Leguas Spanish.

To enter the Bay of San Francisco, keep White Island open with the south shore and run for it until within the harbor, then haul up and anchor abreast of the Town.

The Beginning

Chapter One

MOST NARRATIVES of the settlement of the great Sacramento Valley begin with John Augustus Sutter, and of course this was the beginning of it all as we know it. Here it was that Sutter tied his ships near a gentle rise of land by the bank of the American River, upstream from its confluence with the Sacramento. And here it was he fashioned a private empire complete with standing army and native servants—supreme authority over a wilderness realm which reached as far as the eye could carry, and beyond.

But before Sutter, even before the searching explorations of those from the Old World along the Pacific seaboard—long before both and the new civilizations they brought—there were the Maidu: the people who roamed the valley floor and told their own stories of the origin of the land. Their period, and their legends, tell a complex and separate story.

It might be interesting to recount here, if only with passing briefness, the way the Maidu envisioned the creation of the land they settled and which, in turn, was to be settled by Sutter, and those who followed.

Father to son, the tale was retold:

Before there was man, water covered everything, and there was darkness all around. Upon these waters appeared a raft, and upon the raft, a turtle. From the heavens a rope of feathers was lowered over the raft and down this feeble rope came one who called himself Earth Initiate—one possessed with the power to create worlds. But he would need soil from the bottom of the great waters for this good work, and would the turtle dive and bring from the bottom this stuff of creation? Turtle would. He disappeared beneath the waters and for six years he was not seen, and when he did return to the raft, his claws were empty. He had found the bottom, he said, and he had filled his arms with mud, but it had washed away in the long ascent, and now only a trace was lodged beneath his claws. But he who had descended from the heavens upon that fragile rope of feathers rolled a ball as big as a pebble from that small bit of mud; and as time

The Indians of the Sacramento region came from the Valley Nisenan branch of the Maidu Tribe. Theirs was a natural, pastoral existence, depending on the land, plants, and abundant water for sustenance.

Thomas O. Larkin published this map of the Gold Region
in 1850, basing it on an 1844 survey made by John Bidwell.
Such maps, folded into pocket size, were very popular
after the discovery of gold.

passed, the ball grew larger until one could not span its width with arms out-stretched. Finally it grew into a great sphere. Land rose above the waters and there were mountains all around. And these places may be seen still today.

So spoke the Maidu, father to son.

Thus did they envision the creation of this broad land.

But consider the geologist. He can read his way back to the very begin-nings through clues left in the processes of evolution. He tells us that indeed the valley we know with such familiarity—the Valley of Sutter with its great, broad reaches of fertile plantings, its lush groves, its winding, snaking rivers, its bursting mountains capped at their brows with wrappings of snow—all was once but the bed for the restless ocean. Even the ancestral Sierra ranges rose, only to erode and sink, this more than 140 million years ago, and gave way to the Sierra Sutter found. Evolution had worked its way. With that same creative force which sent the great ranges thrusting skyward out of the molten caverns of the earth, the process also tucked into the crevasses and into the rock, small pockets of yellow mineral. Nameless then, this mineral, and of no worth as barter. The mineral would come to be called gold, and one day would open the great wilderness to massive harvest, and with that harvesting, settlement.

Meanwhile, even as the Sierra was taking form the land was rising and forcing its cover of water back and back. During this period of evolution rain-fall came in endless deluge; and perhaps this deluge, or the great moving gla-ciers of the Ice Ages which followed, cut what geologists now call the Markley Gorge, a ragged wash which scarred the ancient valley floor 1,000 feet deep, and which perhaps constituted a virgin predecessor for what we have come to call the Sacramento. Today this gorge lies buried under almost a mile-deep bath of sediments gathered and washed over the plain in layers over a period of perhaps one million years.

In this age, too, came great quakes when the earth rolled in nervous, heav-ing waves, unsettling and rearranging the terrain time and again. And we know from geological findings that with the rise of new ranges, new land, the seas drew back farther and farther, receding reluctantly and now and then return-ing to lay new claims to old bottoms. But it was only to be driven back anew by thrusting new shoots of land crashing upward.

Thus was the valley created out of a crucible of molten washes of soil, rains beyond imagination, earthquake, glaciers, and flood.

Explorers from the Sea

Exploration and settlement are of two different cuts of cloth, although both come out of the same bolt of goods. It takes a certain breed of man—either questing or escaping—to find, to be consumed with the kind of curiosity which makes him determined to discover on his own what lies beyond the horizon. He has, this man, the instinct to be first to find, to occupy, if only shortly to move on. It takes another breed, the settler, to build upon that discovery, to turn exploration into the more settled stuff of civilization.

The kind of men who first came to command that personal look were a mobile breed—pathfinder, explorer, hunter, trapper, vagrant seaman, car-tographer. He it was who kicked the soil, and in it saw the promise of harvest, and measured with a quick scan of the eye a stand of timber for harvest. Or he envisioned a township where there was only nature's brambles for an earth cover, and the only colony of life in that bramble, wild ants and wild grubs. And he returned to tell others of the promise he saw in the good earth.

In the long history of the exploration preceding settlement under Sutter there were men of the stuff of Cortez who, having conquered Mexico and, excited by rumors of riches to the north, sent out ships to find the El Dorado, only to explore no farther north than what is now La Paz. The discovery of Alta California itself was to be made by Juan Rodríguez Cabrillo in 1542, not by Cortez. And after Cabrillo came Sir Francis Drake and Sebastian Vizcaíno, who sailed the California coastline, but none of whom, most historians agree, found the Golden Gate or discovered the vast reaches beyond that gate—unless it is as some now claim, that Drake actually anchored inside the gate near what is known as Point San Quentin. Others have said the landing was north, near Point Reyes, in what is known today as Drake's Bay.

If the former claimants are right, Drake may have been the first to wonder about the headwaters of the great bay, and about what lay beyond his scan deep

This interior of an Indian home is from an 1844 French publication which described an exploration of the Pacific Coast from 1840 to 1842.

in the interior, in the land Sutter was to settle three centuries later. The exploration of the bay, and the exploration of the waiting Sacramento, however, was to await those who followed Gaspar de Portolá more than two centuries after Cabrillo.

The First Spaniards Overland

After the seaman—and again before Sutter—came the priest, the soldier, trader, and the trapper.

Two hundred years were to pass from the time of Cortez before the church in the seventh decade of the 1700s was to send friars north to Alta California to establish missions and to baptize Indians into the church. First came the settlements in the south, beginning in San Diego. By the year 1833, the missions numbered 21, and the mission populations some 15,000 scattered as far north as Sonoma.

However, the explorations skirted the inland valley. The Indians had earned a reputation for troublemaking by raiding Spanish camps along the coast. They sought horses, and guns, new to the California scene.

Little information was available to the Spanish on the vast interior before 1800. Separate and feeble probes had been made and distant glimpses of the

Tres Picos, or the Buttes, standing in the middle of the Sacramento Valley, figure prominently in Maidu legends and have fascinated travelers through the years by their sudden appearance.

20

valley had been reported by Juan Bautista de Anza, Commandante Pedro Fages, Fray Martin and others, but they were unimpressed. They merely testified again to what was then considered a lack of promise of the interior as a potential place for settlement.

In 1808, however, the tireless explorer and Indian fighter, Gabriel Moraga, did make a personal exploration. He walked the valley from the Calaveras River to the Feather. He became the first European to enter the Sierra, and to be struck with the odd sight of the Sutter Buttes rising abruptly from the valley floor. He crossed the American River, calling it *Las Llagas*, and he first brought the name *Sacramento*—for the Holy Sacrament—to the valley, even though he misplaced the rivers.

Moraga called the snaking Sacramento, then clear and abundant with fish, the Jesus Maria when he came upon its lower reaches. In his confusion, when he reached the abundant Feather he assumed it was the upper Jesus Maria River and so he named a fork to the left the Sacramento, an error which those who followed, and with more patience to trace the flows, corrected.

His report on the interior as a possible mission site?

"I found no site suitable."

Some three years later Padres Abella and Fortuni probed the lower valley, however, and urged establishment of missions. Those in church authority, confused by the new estimate which ran contrary to all of the assessments which came before it, ignored the recommendation.

Then came another turn in the history. In 1821, Mexico finally overcame Spanish rule and established a government independent of the Old World.

Like the Spanish before them, they were not excited about developing the valley, but were determined to keep out intruders. There were rumors of interlopers, and a small group, under Luis Arguello, investigated. They found no trespassing.

What may have been the first non-Spanish expedition to the interior fell to a German in the Russian Imperial Navy. Otto Von Kotzebue who in 1823, so accounts in diaries suggest, sailed well up the Sacramento River, perhaps as far as the American.

Soon a giant in exploration was to come upon the scene: Jedediah Smith, a rustic, Bible-quoting mountain man who thought he may have been in the "Valley of the Bonadventure" when he came upon the country in 1827. Thus he mistakenly thought he may have discovered the legendary master river so many thought surely would be found flowing from the Rocky Mountains into a watershed which eventually would empty into the Pacific. That mythical river was known also as the St. Bonaventura.

Among Smith's campsites, one is thought to be near the campus of Sacramento State University on a beautiful waterway Smith called Wild River. It was from there he set out on what probably was to be the first crossing of the Sierra. Turned back in one probe, he found a path, finally up the Stanislaus River farther south.

Then began the Hudson's Bay exploration. By 1832, John Work and

William A. Jackson's map of the gold rush region published years later indicates the reason for Moraga's confusion over identification of the main stream at the confluence of the Sacramento and Feather Rivers. It would appear, as it did to Moraga, that the Feather and the lower Sacramento (Moraga's Jesus Maria River) are the same river. It also seems that the Sacramento, Moraga's name for the upper reaches of today's river, is a tributary.

The name Buenaventura *attached to both the Sacramento River and the valley was apparently not a Spanish idea. Other European mapmakers and some American maps used this designation. Some of them show the river and the valley accurately. Others, such as this one from Germany in 1834, subscribed to the tales of a master river flowing from the plains west of the Rockies all the way to the Pacific Ocean.*

Jedediah Smith called the Sacramento Valley region Bonadventure. *While using this name, trappers such as Smith and Ogden did not necessarily indicate belief in the inaccurate course of the stream shown here and in other maps, but it does indicate how little information they actually had.*

The sparsely detailed map (below) published with Winterbotham's history in 1795 showed how little real knowledge was at hand concerning the interior of New Albion, also known as Alta California.

Captain B. L. E. Bonneville of the United States Army was an exploring cartographer who helped set the river right on maps, but the acceptance of the Spanish name Sacramento *was not reached as late as Bonneville's 1837 map (right).*

By 1826 and even before, cartographers were willing to assume that so great a bay as the one at San Francisco must be receiving waters from as far away as the Rockies. They sketched a Buenaventura extending to the Utah desert and beyond (below). Once the magnitude of the Sierra Nevada was realized by such men as Jedediah Smith, the river was given a much more accurate course, though men of the Hudson's Bay Company who roamed the Sacramento Valley in the early nineteenth century still called it the Valley of the Buenaventura.

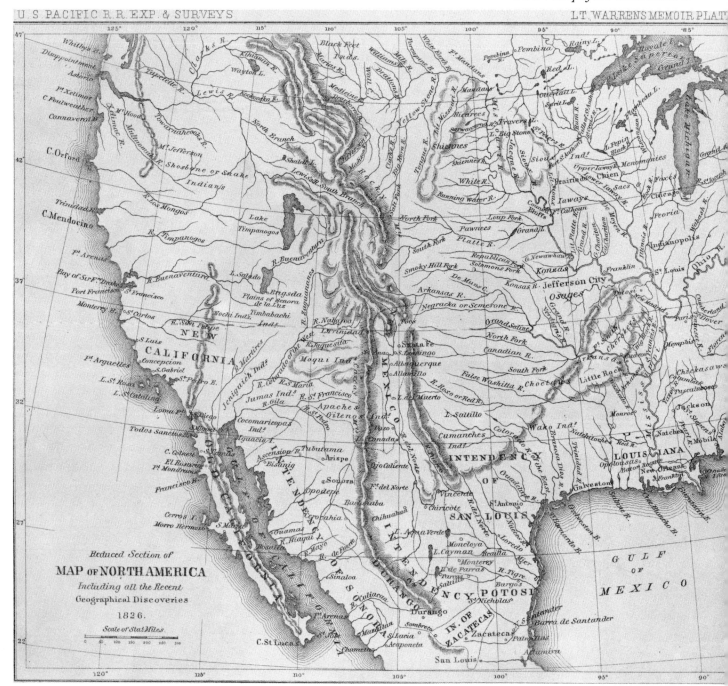

In 1833, John R. Cooper, having married Encarnación Vallejo after his arrival in 1823, requested land in the Sacramento Valley from Mexican officials. The land embraced the Rio Ojotska (now the American) but Cooper never settled on the land. His map (below) is the earliest of the Sacramento region. The request he made left a way open for Sutter just a few years later.

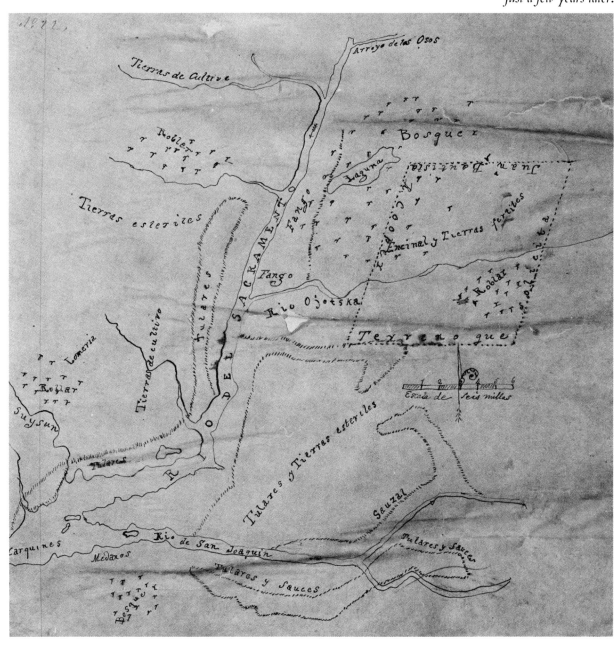

Captain William D. Phelps (above) sailed the cutter *Alert* up the Sacramento in 1837, carrying the first American flag to the interior.

Michael Laframboise had visited the interior valley for the company and the next year Laframboise discovered an easier coast route from Oregon. This led to what Hudson's Bay people came to call "The Southern Party," an enterprise which would be a feature of Hudson's operations on the Pacific slope from 1834 to 1843. During these years, large companies of trappers—the brigades included even women and children—would roam the valley floor for the catch.

An American named John B. R. Cooper came to the valley in 1833, and may have been the first to seek a land grant. He applied to the Mexican government for a grant embracing a Rio Ojotska, on what later was to bear the name American River. Cooper petitioned for land a few miles east of the confluence with the Sacramento not far beyond the site John Sutter was to settle in but a few years.

Cooper forfeited his opportunity, however. He failed to implement the grant.

There were probes, too, on the river feeding into the great delta. In 1837, British and American ships, so records bear witness, penetrated the Sacra-

A detachment from Lieutenant Charles Wilkes' United States Pacific Exploring Expedition made an overland sweep of the Sacramento Valley in 1841. Some of its members met Sutter at the fort on August 23, 1841.

mento. W. D. Phelps, aboard the American cutter *Alert*, was the first to carry the flag of the United States to the waters which passed by the bank near the rise Sutter soon would settle; and Captain Edward Belcher wrote that he took long boats from *HMS Sulphur* some 100 miles upstream on the Sacramento the same year.

The valley now had felt the foot of exploration and its promise was becoming legend. Mexican authority was aware of this, and in the councils of that authority there were discussions on how the trespasser could be discouraged—and the empire preserved for Mexico. Had no sense of this urgency existed, perhaps John Sutter would have been denied when he petitioned the Mexican governor for land.

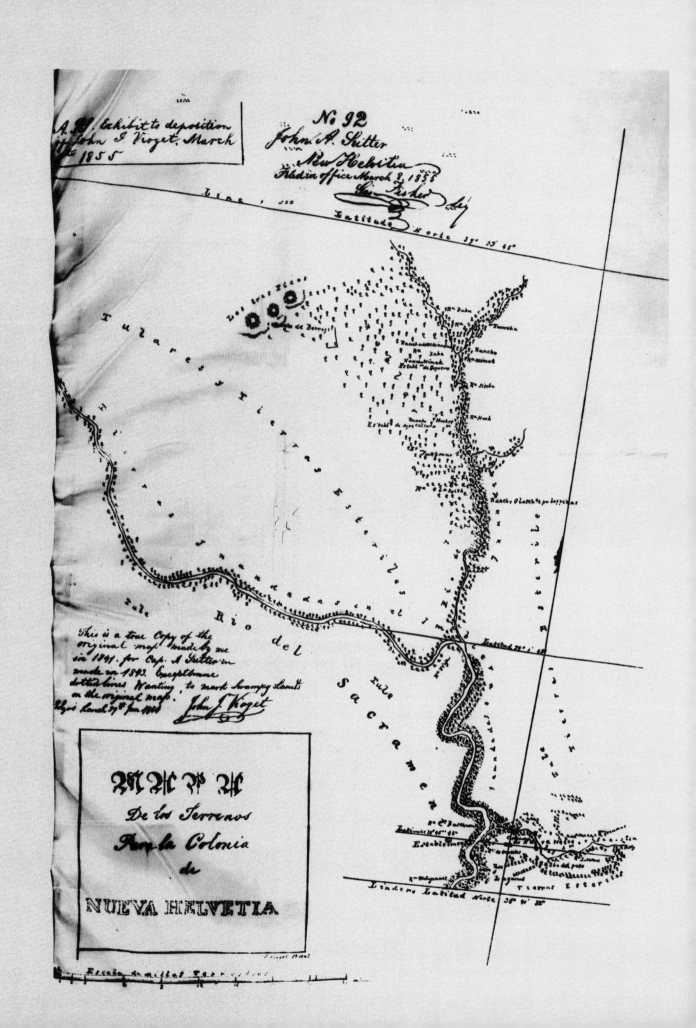

The Sutter Years

Chapter Two

JOHN AUGUSTUS SUTTER the man is almost as big as John Augustus Sutter the legend. And as filled with contradictions.

To understand Sutter the empire builder it is necessary first to come to know Sutter the man.

To begin at the beginning:

Sutter, who had so much to do with settling the Far West in the New World, was a native of the Old World.

He was born February 23, 1803, in a small Black Forest town called Kandern within territory belonging to the Margrave of Baden, in Bavaria; and he spent his early life in that area and in nearby Switzerland.

At 16, he became an apprentice to a bookseller in Basel, in Switzerland; at 19, he became a clerk for a cloth merchant in Aarburg, then for a grocer in Burgdorf.

He married rather late for his generation—at 25—and to support his wife he established a clothing and yardage business. It failed, perhaps because of the same personal frailties in an otherwise strong man which were to plague him even as an empire builder.

To quote Erwin G. Gudde, historian, Sutter was inclined toward "grand living, a penchant for making lavish promises, open-handed liberality, and an incapability to calculate and attend to business."

Even his motives in leaving Switzerland for the New World may not have been the purest. Some accounts suggest that when he left his wife and four children behind in 1834 to sail to New York, he was deeply in debt—that he faced pauper's prison.

For whatever reason, he embarked for the New World and a new life, spending his first winter in St. Louis. In two years, he had entered the Santa Fe trail trade; and it was this exposure which brought him word that California offered fantastic rewards to the settler.

He thought upon the possibility, and the ambition evolved. He would go

So many portraits of Sutter in his middle and late years have obscured the look of the younger man. In this portrait of Sutter in 1839 when he had just arrived, he has the appearance of a man of energy and determination.

Sutter's land was granted from an 1841 map drawn by John Vioget, who also drew this version in 1855. The land stretched over 11 leagues.

to California; he would seek a land grant from the Mexican government; he would build a colony for migrating Swiss and other Europeans, a New Helvetia.

Inquiring, Sutter learned of only two parties who ever had reached California over the massive Sierra—Jedediah Smith and Joseph Walker. With all of its demands, the Sierra route was not for Sutter; he chose an alternative, the north.

He left Missouri with a company under the command of a Captain Tripps of the American Fur Company, and remained with this company until he reached the Wind River Valley in Wyoming. There he formed a party of six men. They deserted him in the Willamette Valley in Oregon. He proceeded to Vancouver. There were no ships immediately sailing to Monterey, where he could petition the Mexican Government for land. He would take a ship, instead, to the Sandwich Islands in the Pacific and there, he was told, he should have no difficulty getting passage to California. Such was not the case, however. He was forced to wait in the Islands five months. Finally he negotiated to take charge of a brig, the *Clementine*, bound for Sitka, Alaska—very much out of his way—where he would sell the cargo, then proceed southward to Monterey.

Enroute from Sitka, Sutter's small brig ran into storms and difficulties. His supplies low, his ship in danger, he put in at Yerba Buena (San Francisco) where Mexican officials, agitated, told him he would have to proceed on to Monterey, for Monterey was the only port in Mexican California which would accept a foreign ship. He was allowed two days, however, to take on provisions and make repairs.

There was a reason for the concern. Suspicious of foreign ambitions to secure a beachhead on its California holdings, Mexico had imposed strict regulations governing the receiving of foreign ships.

Sutter Finds His Land

Arriving in Monterey, Captain Sutter gained audience with Governor Alvarado and told him of his ambition to establish, on new land, an empire of civilization. Alvarado was impressed. The Indians of the north long had been troublesome to the Mexicans and Alvarado saw in Sutter an opportunity to establish an outpost in the remote regions of the Sacramento Valley without committing any of his own troops to secure that settlement. Sutter was told to explore the rivers and to take possession of any location "pleasing" to him. Then he was to return to Monterey a year later to have his title confirmed. All in all, a very satisfactory arrangement—to Alvarado as well as to Sutter.

The commitment made, the prospect of title to a vast land consumed Sutter's days in preparation. He proceeded to San Francisco Bay and Yerba Buena. He was behind his schedule by months, but finally he made arrangements for three boats through Yerba Buena merchants Spear and Hinkley: the schooner *Isabella*, a yacht said to have belonged once to the king of the Sandwich Islands, and a small pinnace.

While awaiting the outfitting of his small exploration fleet, Sutter established contacts which would prove helpful. He visited Mariano Vallejo, the

Russians at Fort Ross, and Ignacio Martinez, whose rancho was near the Straits of Carquinez.

Sutter completely won the small Yerba Buena settlement; he was given every encouragement. While he could find none who had ventured up-bay, into the delta, and beyond into the area he intended to command for his own, he left with their good wishes. Perhaps because they felt they might never see him again; there was no gainsaying the future; life in the unknown and the unsettled is not predictable.

So Sutter set out with three German carpenters he had brought from the Islands, several sailors to man the three craft, two mechanics he encouraged to join him during his stay in Yerba Buena, and eight Kanakas—Hawaiians— whom journals suggest were "given" to Sutter by King Kamehameha while he waited for passage in the Islands.

It was August 1, 1839. Almost 300 years—297 to be exact—had passed since Juan Cabrillo pioneered the sea passage north along the California coast; now Sutter embarked from Yerba Buena and for the delta and thence north, up the Sacramento and into the wilderness beyond to take of it what he wished. He had Alvarado's promise he might command 11 Spanish leagues—or 76 square miles—of any unoccupied land "convenient" to Sutter. He would, he was determined, establish a New Helvetia; he would be its master.

Perhaps it would be effective here to quote Sutter's own recollections of his voyage up the Sacramento. This account, in his own handwriting, was found in his papers after his death. No reconstruction approaches the lean drama of his phraseology. It follows:

It took me eight days before I could find the entrance to the Sacramento, as it is very deceiving and very easy to pass by, how it happened to several Officers of the Navy afterwards which refused to take a pilot. About 10 miles below Sacramento City I fell in with the first Indians which was all armed & painted & looked very hostile, they was about 200 armed Men, as some of them understood a little Spanish I could make a Kind of treaty with them, and the two which understood Spanish came with me, and made me a little better acquainted with the Country. all other Indians on the up River hided themselves in the Bushes, and on the Mouth of Feather River they runned all away so soon they discovered us. I was examining the Country a little further up with a Boat, while the larger Crafts let go their Ankers, on my return, all the white Men came to me and asked me, how much longer I intended to travell with them in such a Wilderness.

The following Morning I gave Orders to return, and entered in the American River, landed . . . on the 12th Augt. 1839. Gave Orders to get every thing on Shore, pitch the tents and mount the 3 Cannons, called the White Men, and told them that all those which are not contented could leave on board the Isabella, next Morning, and that I could settle with them immediately and remain alone with the Canaca's, of 6 Men 3 remained, and 3 of them I gave passage to Yerbabuena.

After reaching the Feather and turning about, Sutter picked the entrance to the American at its confluence with the Sacramento and, his landing selected, he turned to the task of setting up a base camp. For some days he surveyed the

Jared Dixon Sheldon was a Vermonter who came to California in 1832 or 1840. He was an early Sutter neighbor. At one time, under threat of jail for debts, Sheldon lived with Indians and led raids against the Mexicans, who offered him amnesty if he quit, and even granted him a rancho.

The
Building Year

31

land, selecting a gently rising knoll well back from both rivers, as the place to build his settlement.

First came his adobe residence, then one by one additional buildings as his enterprise expanded: a blacksmith shop, a carpenter shop, a mill room, storerooms, guest rooms and, yes, a saloon. For a time he maintained a distillery and served from it generously. However, when he found that work on his fort was coming to a standstill he quickly put an end to his free service of spirits.

He built of the materials at hand: out of brick webbed with straw from his threshings, the Indians mixing work with play by dancing in the brick troughs to mix straw and mud, and out of logs roughly hewn. To give him security, he built outside walls, producing an enclosed settlement—a fort in the best sense of the word. His bastion measured some 200 feet square, the walls were some 12 to 16 feet high, and provided two emplacements for cannon—one in the east, one in the west.

It emerged, the fort, as a wilderness outpost, as a point of security for travel in an otherwise untamed land. It stood for something more. It stood as testament to the fact that development of the vast interior of this abundantly rich valley was inevitable.

Ignacio Martinez, who operated a ranch near the Carquinez Straits and with whom Sutter had established contact while waiting for his ships to be prepared in Yerba Buena for the sailing upstream, was Sutter's main supplier in the early critical months. Martinez may, moreover, have been the first in California to complain of Sutter's tardiness in making payment. Through his lifetime, this characteristic was to flaw the Sutter reputation.

Among his early visitors were Peter Lassen who was to become a distinguished pioneer, and William Wiggins who arrived at Sutter's settlement in August, 1840. But not all who followed were to Sutter's liking. He complained that too many who stopped to accept his hospitality were "rabble." He gave these short shrift.

The Indians Sutter found in the broad valley were at once curious and apprehensive, which made for a certain hostility. By name, they were the Valley Nisenan, a branch of the Maidu, who lived rather primitively in huts made of stitched saplings, in small settlements, perhaps with open fires burning in lean-tos.

They may have been dulled, their initiative and their stamina sapped, by the generous bounty so easy to their reach—in vegetation and in game and in fish—and by the relatively mild seasons. Life for them was not nearly so harsh, for example, as in settlements in sterner climes and on lands more sparse in their offerings.

Two villages are known to have existed in the immediate Sacramento area in the early settlement: Pushune, near the confluence of the American and the Sacramento rivers, and Kadema, located near what is the Watt Avenue Bridge today. To the north were the Hoks, a Nisenan village on the Feather, and namesake for the sanctuary to which Sutter would retreat when the Argonauts tramped down his lands and stole his cattle and vandalized his fort. That sanctuary: Hock Farm.

They were simple people, these Indians native to this rich region. They

William Daylor was an Englishman who worked as a cook for Sutter at the fort in 1840. Daylor married Jared Sheldon's sister.

were hunting and fishing tribes but ate, in great measure, of acorns, seeds, and roots. They wore scant clothing. The men seldom wore so much as a loin cloth. When the weather would turn cold, they fashioned aprons or capes of tules and sometimes sought warmth in a blanket of duck feathers, or deerskin robes, or in mantles of rabbit fur.

Their origin? Most accounts trace the origin of California Indians to migration from the Asiatic climes in the Dark Ages, before the period of so-called Enlightenment; the Sacramento Valley Indian is numbered among these.

Peaceful though they might have been, they gave Sutter difficulties. Sutter wrote in his recollections:

The Indians was first troublesome, and came frequently and would it not have been for the Cannons they would have killed us for sake of my property, which they liked very much, and this intention they had very often, how they confessed to me afterwards, when on good terms. I had a large Bull Dog which saved my life 3 times, when they came slyly near the house in the Night, he got hold of them and barked most severly. In a short time removed my Camps on the very spot where now the Ruins of Sutters fort stands, made acquaintance with a few Indians which came to work for a short time making Adobes, and the Canacas was building 3 grass houses, like it is customary on the Sandwich Islands. Before I came up here, I purchased Cattle & Horses on the Rancho of Senor Martinez, and had great difficulties & trouble to get them up, and received them at last on the 22 October 1839. Not less than 8 Men, wanted to be in the party, as they was afraid of the Indians, and had good reasons to be so.

Before I got the Cattle we was hunting Deer & Elk etc and soon afterwards to safe the Cattle as I had then only about 500 head, 50 horses & a manada of 25 mares. One year that is in the fall 1840, I bought 1000 head of cattle of Don Antonio Sunol and many more of Don Joaquin Gomez and others. In the fall of 1839 I built an Adobe house, covered with Tule and two other small buildings which in the middle of the fort, they was afterwards destroyed by fire . . . At the same time we cut a Road through the Woods where the City of Sacramento stand, then we made the New Embarcadero.

In the spring of 1840, the Indians began to be troublesome all around me, Killing and Wounding Cattle stealing horses, and threatening to attack us en Mass, I was obliged to make campaigns against them and punish them severely, a little later about 2 a 300 was approaching and got United on Cosumne River, but I was not waiting for them. left a small Garrison at home, canons & other Arms loaded, and left with 6 brave men & 2 Baquero's in the night, and took them by surprise at Day light. the fighting was a little hard, but after having lost about 30 men, they was willing to make a treaty with me, and after this leson they behaved very well, and became my best friends and Soldiers, with which I has been assisted to conquer the whole Sacramento and a part of the San Joaquin Valley.

Governor Alvarado had told Sutter that it would be necessary for him to become a citizen of Mexico in order to receive any grant of land. Therefore, Sutter made such an application, which was formally granted on August 29, 1840, along with appointment as judge and representative of the "Government at the Frontiers of the Rio Sacramento."

By now there were some 20 men working at New Helvetia in addition to a considerable number of Indians. By the next June, in 1841, Sutter received

Fort Ross was sold to John Sutter when the Russians gave up their California ambitions in 1841. Sutter removed almost everything and the fort began its quiet decay on the ruggedly beautiful California coast.

formal transfer of title of the 11 leagues of land, or some 44,000 acres. Truly now he had empire. His property reached, according to the actual wording of the grant, from the Three Peaks and latitude 39 degrees, 41 minutes, 45 seconds on the north, down to 38 degrees, 49 minutes, 32 seconds on the south; and from the Sacramento River on the west to the "margins of the river De Los Plumas" on the east.

He was, moreover, to expand his empire. While he was at work directing construction of his fort, the Russian governor attached to Fort Ross on the coast paid Sutter an official visit.

The czarists were giving up their California settlement, he disclosed, ending some 28 years of Russian occupation at the fort. He blamed crop failures and logistics and the difficulty of maintaining a fort so far removed from the touchstones of Sitka and Russia.

The Russians, he said, would be pleased to sell Sutter their holdings. He would rather do business with Sutter, he said, than with the Mexican government. He stipulated what was a fair price: some $30,000. Sutter accepted, gratefully; it was a remarkable offer. He immediately transferred from Fort Ross much of the fort's physical property, along with livestock and a schooner which he renamed the *Sacramento*. He lost about 100 of a herd of some 2,000 cattle, horses, mules and sheep, on the drive from Fort Ross to Sacramento; but, frugal in small things, he salvaged the hides. Now he had another creditor who was to become impatient.

Neighbors, Visitors, Empire

Sutter had become a force and an authority in his own right. By the end of the first year, his name was becoming widely known. He had complete authority over his domain. He was general over a private army; he married, he buried, he hired, he fired, he rewarded, he punished. In short, his power was absolute.

A tannery rose near the bank of the American almost at the point where he first stepped ashore. He had planted his first crops, had created a pasture for his herd, had cut out a path to the bank of the Sacramento, where the Embarcadero was to rise.

Soon began the flow of visitors. In August of 1840, he had entertained Lassen and Wiggins. In August of 1841 he entertained new arrivals who had come by boat. Lieutenant C. J. Ringgold of the United States Navy was attached to the Wilkes Exploring expedition and is remembered in Californiana for his magnificent drawings and maps of the delta and river waterways.

The first organized overland party arrived in 1841 also. Included were John Bidwell, destined to become a close friend and a trusted lieutenant of Sutter and a valley pioneer in his own right; Charles M. Weber, who later founded Stockton; and Henry Huber, an agriculturist who became superintendent of farming operations at New Helvetia.

The Indians who watched Sutter make the passage up the river in August, 1839, must have felt new apprehension with each new arrival. The fort had become entrenched, a visible rootshoot of permanence. The Indians must have sensed life by the river, which had remained unchanged, father to son, for so many generations, never could be the same again, for more new arrivals came to stay.

John Sinclair settled just north of Sutter in 1842. Sutter gave considerable land to Nicolaus Allgier, for whom Nicolaus on the Feather River is named.

He also gave property to Pablo Guitierez above Allgier, and to John Smith along the Yuba. Theodore Cordua is said to have leased a parcel of Sutter's land at the junction of the Yuba and Feather Rivers to start a settlement called New Mecklenburg, now Marysville.

And the Sutter at the height of his authority? A visitor, James C. Ward, gave this account of Sutter as he recalled him:

I passed the evening of my arrival, after supper, in his company. His manners are polished and the impression he makes on every one is very favorable. In figure he is of medium height, rather stout, but well made. His head is round, features regular, with smiling and agreeable expression; complexion healthy and roseate. He wears his hair cut close and his moustache trimmed short, a la militaire. He dressed very neatly in frock coat, pantaloons, and cap of blue, and with his gold-headed malacca in hand, you would rather suppose him prepared for a saunter on the Boulevards than a consultation with Simplon, his Indian alcalde, about hands required for the day's work, or ox teams to be dispatched here and there.

Witness another account of life at the fort, written by a young Swedish scholar, in 1843—only four years after Sutter established his settlement:

Against the walls [of the fort] on the inside are erected the store-houses of the establishment; also a distillery to make spirits from wheat and grapes, together with shops for coopers, blacksmiths, saddlers, granaries, and huts for laborers. At the gateway is always stationed a servant, armed as a sentinel. I found Captain Sutter busily employed in distributing orders for the day. He received me with great hospitality, and made me feel on the instant, perfectly at home under his roof. The magical sound of the drum had gathered together several hundred Indians who flocked to their morning meal preparatory to the labors of the day, reaping wheat. The morning

Arriving at Sutter's Fort on Christmas Day, 1845, Lansford W. Hastings later helped Sutter and Bidwell lay out Sutterville.

35

Kit Carson (left) and John C. Frémont posed for this formal portrait years after their historic arrival at Sutter's Fort in 1844.

meal over, they filed off to the field in a kind of military order, armed with a sickle and hook.

The raising of wheat, corn, horses and cattle constitutes the principal business of Captain Sutter; but he has realized considerable income from the salmon fisheries of the rivers, the fish being unequalled in flavor, and found in the greatest abundance. He also organized extensive hunting and trapping expeditions for the skins of the beaver, otter, elk, deer and antelope, but in this he was greatly interfered with by the Hudson's Bay Company, who sent their hunters upon his grounds. He complained to the proper authorities but they paid no attention to the matter . . . He retaliated by erecting a large distillery, with the product of which he secretly purchased from the hunters of the company the greater part of their furs, and managed to make more by the operation than if he had kept up a large hunting establishment of his own.

As the fort began to prosper, as demands upon him began to increase with his expanded holdings, Sutter looked beyond his fort for a retreat from the pressures.

He selected a picturesque piece of acreage on the Feather near an Indian Village called Hok, and there built a farm—calling it Hock Farm. It was to become Sutter's last refuge in the bitter days ahead when his empire would be lost to the Argonauts, a vision mercifully spared Sutter in his years of conquest.

By 1844 New Helvetia had become a stable frontier outpost. The fact it was the only place in Alta California where foreigners might find refuge was to become significant in the eventual Americanization of California.

Lieutenant John Frémont had been mapping and exploring the West for the United States. Without explanation, he had crossed the Sierra—this in the dead of winter.

These were the conditions Frémont and his men faced crossing the Sierra in winter. As an Indian told them, they found nothing but "rock upon rock . . . snow upon snow."

With Frémont was a guide already widely known as a frontiersman, Kit Carson. The party made it to Sutter's Fort, badly in need of aid and supplies. There the expedition was outfitted anew from Sutter's stores and herds, a generous act that Mexican authorities, now increasingly concerned over holding California against intruders, would have frowned upon. It might even have jeopardized Sutter's influence and position in Mexican favors.

Really, Sutter's position was precarious from the beginning. His fort, his settlement, naturally would attract others. And the greater the migrations, the more serious the threat to Mexican authority as well as his own.

It was a political fact of life, moreover, that the United States could not forever live with a Mexican partition blocking off its access to the Pacific. The United States, by the time of Sutter's emergence, had determined in its own inner councils that one way or another, it must eventually have California. It was politically as much a part of this nation's "manifest destiny" to possess California and bring it to the Union as it was manifest destiny in Thomas Jefferson's time to secure from France the vast territory to the west of the emerging nation.

Sutter's situation worsened when he became caught in the middle, a pawn between contesting forces within the Mexican government. He backed the unpopular Governor Manuel Micheltorena when Californians Alvarado and Castro led a coup which overthrew the government dispatched from Mexico City—and landed Sutter in jail. Before the deciding battle, Micheltorena had signed documents issuing Sutter the so-called Sobrante grant of 22 leagues of new land and confirming the 1841 grant. It followed then that Micheltorena's defeat placed all Sutter's holdings in jeopardy. However, for reasons not entirely clear, the new government not only granted him his freedom, but also honored the land grants the former governor Alvarado had granted Sutter.

Micheltorena had been busy giving away land in the Sacramento Valley to others during the last months of his administration. His actions seemed a kind of recognition that growth, after Sutter, was inevitable.

To complete the record of history in land grants significant to this area, there were these holdings granted by Governor Micheltorena in 1844 and 1845:

    Rancho Omochumnes on the north Cosumnes, five leagues
    Chabolla, south Cosumnes, eight leagues
    Rancho Rio de los Americanos, on the south reaches of the American, eight leagues
    Rancho Cosumnes, on the south Cosumnes, 11 leagues
    Rancho Cacadores on the northwest Cosumnes, four leagues
    Rancho del Paso on the northwest American, 11 leagues
    Rancho de San Juan on the American, east of Del Paso, four and one-half leagues

and, of course, the Sobrante grant to Sutter, constituting the 22 leagues.

John Bidwell also applied for, and received from Micheltorena, a grant for 17,726 acres he called Rancho Los Ulpinos, in November, 1844. Located in what is now Solano County, along the west bank of the Sacramento River near Rio Vista, Bidwell built an adobe house and put workmen there; but he

John Bidwell was in the first party to reach California by the overland route; a gruelling trip in 1841. He became friend and employee to John Sutter and a pioneer in his own right. Chico was founded on his rancho, where he lived on until 1900.

Barber and Baker produced this lithograph of the dramatic flag raising at Sutter's Fort in 1846. Sutter told of firing the cannon until windows shattered, but he said he was anxious to get back to business as usual.

Sutter's ambitious plans for Sutterville are shown in this plat found in an 1849 German book telling the wonders of California to potential gold seekers. When Sacramento was founded, Sutterville was doomed, though Sutter's choice was wiser because it was on higher ground.

PLAN VON SUTTERSVILLE.

NORD HÄLFTE

SÜD HÄLFTE

Cedern Strasse (Cedar Street)

Grüne Strasse (Green Str.)

Kirche

Fichten Strasse (Pine Str.)

Eichen Strasse (Oak Str.)

Stadthaus

Läden

Markt Strasse

Markt-Platz

Öffentlicher Platz

Fleisch

Akazien Strasse (Locust Street)

Künste Vierte Dritte Zweite Erste Strasse

Wasser Strasse

Elisen Strasse

Kirche

Kirch Strasse

SACRAMENTO FLUSS.

Kastanien Strasse (Chesnut Str.)

While Sutterville never achieved its projected stature, it was an active community during the Gold Rush and for a few years afterward. George V. Cooper caught the activity in 1849 in this view in Lett's California Illustrated.

Our tents.

19 Sutters Fort in
April 1849.

The fort built by John Sutter had stood on the little knoll for nearly a decade when the Argonauts arrived. The fort fascinated them and it provided an unexpected bit of stability in the wild country. Artists, too, were drawn to the scene as they passed by.

The sketch by William Rich Hutton (above) was done in 1849. Hutton, an engineer, showed his own tents in the left foreground. Renowned George V. Cooper did the drawing at upper right and William McIlvaine's quiet and soft tone are evident in the work at the lower right.

40

never lived on the property himself. He sold lots from it, however, even though his grant prohibited such sale; and in 1866, title was confirmed by the United States government to protect those to whom Bidwell sold the parcels.

The Sutter who returned to the fort after the ill-fated campaign in support of Micheltorena was a far more humble figure than the one who had set out in pomp and optimism just a few weeks earlier. His own immodest assessment at the beginning is evident in this proud description of his own forces when he led them to San Jose: "The whole country stood in awe of me. Such a military force had never before been seen in this part of the world."

A few weeks later it was a dejected general who returned after the defeat at Cahuenga, somehow still holding his freedom and his lands—even the last-minute Sobrante Grant from the deposed and unpopular Micheltorena. The aura of infallibility, so important to a rule in the primitive frontier, was jeopardized. The Sutter image had been tarnished and even though he was sure time would bring its healing influences, the disintegration of his personal empire lay ahead beyond his power to stem.

Seeds of Disintegration

Less than two years later, California was to become a territory of the United States as a result of the Mexican War. Manifest Destiny, the vision of a nation spanning the Atlantic to the Pacific—and with this spanning of a nation, the uniting of a people—was nearing its completion.

A casual reading of the history suggests that while the valley never was to be turned into a battleground in the struggle for California, the fact that Sutter's Fort existed and constituted the one place sympathizers might take refuge, was pertinent.

At one time those anxious to discourage immigration and strengthen California as a more or less independent entity within the framework of Mexico, made an attractive offer to purchase Sutter's Fort and holdings. General José Castro and others arrived at the fort in November of 1845 to arrange transferral for $100,000 and other considerations. Sutter described his decision later by saying,

Thereupon I withdrew to my office in the same building and held a consultation with Bidwell, Reading, and Locker. I told them what I had been offered for the establishment and they all thought that it was a very large sum. After they had discussed the matter for some time, their thoughts turned naturally upon their own interest. "What shall we do?" they said. "And what will all the settlers in the valley do if you abandon us to the Mexicans?" This brought about my decision. I felt that I was in duty bound to continue my protection of the immigrants. Had it not been for this consideration, I should have accepted the Mexican offer. Often I have regretted not having sold New Helvetia at that time, because for this great sacrifice I have been rewarded with nothing but ingratitude.

Indeed he must have regretted his decision in the next years, when Argonauts tramped low his fields, stole his cattle (in one day, five men in the first year of the Gold Rush were to slay some $60,000 worth of Sutter herds) and turned his fort into a wayside on the Gold Trail.

The Bear Flag flew over Sutter's Fort for a few weeks in 1846 when Frémont entrusted some Mexican prisoners to Sutter, who treated them as guests.

But before that, on June 16, 1846, while Frémont was conveniently camped near the Buttes, American settlers, alarmed at Mexican threats and led by Ide, Semple, and others, proclaimed the Bear Flag Republic at Sonoma. It was Kit Carson who informed those at Sutter's Fort about the revolt in Sonoma, but only hours before the revolutionaries arrived demanding use of Sutter's prison.

Sutter reluctantly granted the wish. He was to write later: "The Bear Flag was raised at Sonoma by a band of robbers under Fremont's command."

The prisoners included General Mariano Vallejo, Colonel Prudon, Jacob Leese, Salvador Vallejo and Julio Carillo. They were Sutter's neighbors; so, while confining them, he treated them as guests. Frémont, all military with no give, was reported to have expressed disgust with Sutter for what he considered a breach of conduct; but Sutter remained host and not jailor.

Rumors the United States had gone to war with Mexico were abundant. But it was not until July 11, 1846 that Lieutenant Joseph Warren Revere, a nephew of Paul, the famed Lexington rider, sent a flag of the United States to the fort. When morning came, John Sutter once again raised a new flag on his staff, and ordered cannons fired as the Stars and Stripes replaced the short-lived bear emblem.

In its short life in the wilderness, the fort had flown three flags—those of Mexico, the Bear Flag Republic, and the United States of America.

The long expected and even long awaited war between Mexico and the United States had erupted early in 1846. It began in Texas over issues peculiar to that territory, but in the mysterious world of international politics, California also had become important to American security. It was no accident that both land and sea forces of the United States stood nearby and ready when word came that open conflict had begun. Commodore Sloat's fleet had been in

Mariano G. Vallejo was respected by both his Mexican countrymen and by the Americans who overthrew him in northern California, where he was Commandante.

43

the region of the California coast for months, and Frémont's exploratory company, forerunner of the California Battalion, had been lingering since spring in spite of an outright confrontation with Mexican forces at Hawk's Peak.

As for Sutter's interests, the war was distant and just another disruptive incident in the captain's quest for personal empire. The battles took place mostly in the South, and except for an annoying lack of manpower due to the desertion of his men to join the war, the fort's principal war role was that of unfurling the United States flag near the main gate.

Sloat declared California annexed to the Union in 1846 when he landed in Monterey, but it did not become official until nearly two years later with the signing of the Treaty of Guadalupe Hidalgo. However, the treaty came as an anticlimax at Sutter's Fort. Since its beginning, the fort had been the most American of California settlements and the war served only to emphasize the point. The coming of the Great Democracy, as some historians like to put it, did not extinguish Sutter's hopes, still held deeply, for personal empire. The fact is that there was no strength Sutter could mount, no persuasion of heart,

Lieutenant Joseph Warren Revere, a descendent of Paul Revere, made this sketch of Sutter's Fort in 1846. The fort was even then the center of activity.

no personal influence upon history that could stem the inevitable settlement of the valley he founded. His time of personal empire was now limited.

A kind of democracy had been introduced to the fort by 1846. In September of that year, residents of the fort selected a magistrate in what may have been the first election in the interior's new history. The winner was John Sinclair, by a vote of 15 out of 24 ballots cast.

But there were seeds of disintegration beginning to appear in the fortunes of the fort. Sutter had lost many of his workers to the war in the south. So when the Mormon Battalion with 240 men arrived at the fort, en route to the Great Salt Lake, the new arrivals were welcomed, for there was need for more hands. About this same time, Sam Brannan, also a Mormon and a San Francisco merchant, arrived to survey business possibilities at the fort. He was singularly impressed with Sutter and instinctively respected the man who had turned a wilderness into an outpost, and had marshalled forces to command it. So impressed was he that he established a store outside the fort, and called it C. C. Smith and Company to distinguish it from his Brannan and Co. operation in the Bay Area.

Perhaps Brannan admired Sutter, but Sutter did not admire Brannan. In only a short time they would become deadly rivals in business, with Brannan building up the Embarcadero—and becoming California's first millionaire— giving Sutter harsh, new competition, and in the end killing off Sutter's dream to found a city with himself its namesake downstream on the Sacramento where flood was not so great a threat.

Looking to the future, Sutter was planning a sawmill. He sent his trusted associate and friend, James Wilson Marshall of New Jersey, into the hills to find a site. The year: 1847.

What happened next is history.

Sam Brannan, called California's first millionaire, opened a store at the fort but later he and Sutter parted because of Brannan's influence in building up Sacramento City instead of Sutterville.

Sutters-Fort.

Nach dem Sacramento.

Reisebilder eines Heimgekehrten

von

CARL MEYER.

Ich höre sie rutschen, ich höre sie ziehen. Gold. Gold. Gold!

AARAU

Druck u. Verlag von H. R. Sauerländer.

Sutters-Mühle.

Gold and the City

IT WAS JANUARY, 1848. James Wilson Marshall had been sent to the Sierra foothills by Sutter to put up a sawmill. A yellow flake, glittering in the sand of the shallow channel caught Marshall's eye while he was inspecting a raceway. He picked it up. He rolled it in his fingers. He bit into it: it had, as it has been said, the look and feel and taste of gold.

That night, he boiled the flake in a cookup of homemade soap. If it lost its luster in this caustic test, it probably would not be gold. If it retained its color, it probably would be. Its color survived.

Four nights later he rode into the fort on horseback. As John Sutter tells it in his own recollections:

Marshall arrived in the evening, it was raining very heavy, but he told me that he came on important business, after we was alone in a private room he showed me the first Specimens of Gold, that is he was not certain if it was Gold or not, but he thought it might be; immediately I made the proof and found that it was Gold, I told him even that most of all is 23 Carat Gold; he wished that I should come up with him immediately, but I told him that I have to give first my orders to the people in all my factories and shops.

In an entry of his recollections dated February 1, Sutter said:

Left for the Sawmill attended by a Baquero (Olimpio) was absent 2d, 3d, 4th, & 5th, I examined myself everything and picked up a few Specimens of Gold myself in the tail race of the Sawmill, this Gold and others which Marshall and some of the other laborers gave to me (it was found while in my employ and Wages) I told them that I would a ring got made of it so soon as the Goldsmith would be here. I had a talk with my employed people all at the Sawmill, I told them that as they do know now that this Metal is Gold, I wished that they would do me the great favor and keep it secret only 6 weeks, because my large Flour Mill at Brighton would have been in Operation in such a time, which undertaking would have been a fortune to me, and unfortunately the people would not keep it secret, and so I lost on this Mill at the lowest calculation about $25,000.

James Marshall was establishing Sutter's mill when he found a piece of yellow mineral he thought might be gold. Sutter confirmed Marshall's opinion.

Carl Meyer's 1850 account of Gold Country, Nach dem Sacramento, *had a cover which took him through the tropics to Sutter's Fort and into the Sierra. Many such books were done at the time.*

Second Street in 1849 was sketched by Robert Fulton and sent home to New Hampshire. The exact location is vague, but the group of businesses is thought to be between K and L.

There are accounts, moreover, that Sutter and Marshall probed more than the millrace for color, that they made a quick inspection of the streams, nearby, and found gold not only in the streambed but "in the bed of every little dried up creek and ravine."

Gold in California!

There was one certainty: such a secret could not be kept for long. For one, Sam Brannan, a businessman alert to every opportunity, picked up the report. He quickly grasped the promise of merchandising.

Some accounts suggest he hit the streets of San Francisco, hat in one hand and a bottle with specimens of gold in the other, shouting: "Gold! Gold! Gold, from the American River!" Some have speculated whether the gold in the bottle actually came from the Coloma Country or from his private vault. Whichever, it made for a good show, and it did excite the interest Brannan set out to arouse.

The first newspaper account was published March 15 in the *Californian* in San Francisco. It read: "Gold Mine Found—In the newly-made race-way of the saw-mill recently erected by Captain Sutter, on the American Fork, gold

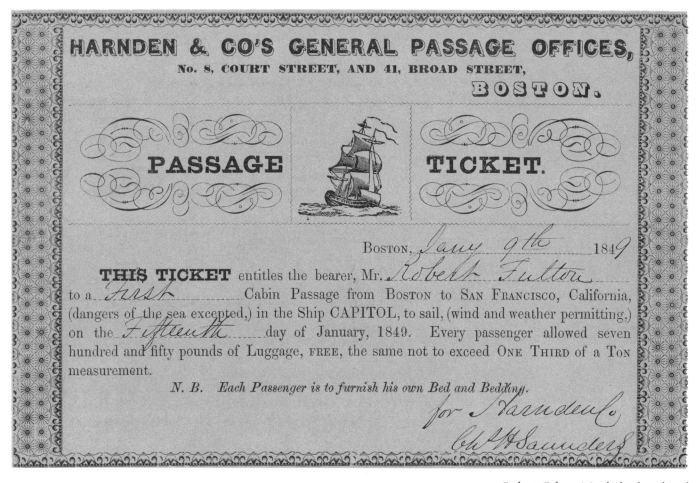

HARNDEN & CO'S GENERAL PASSAGE OFFICES,

No. 8, COURT STREET, AND 41, BROAD STREET,

BOSTON.

PASSAGE TICKET.

BOSTON, *Jany 9th* 1849

THIS TICKET entitles the bearer, Mr. *Robert Fulton*
to a *First* Cabin Passage from BOSTON to SAN FRANCISCO, California,
(dangers of the sea excepted,) in the Ship CAPITOL, to sail, (wind and weather permitting,)
on the *Fifteenth* day of January, 1849. Every passenger allowed seven
hundred and fifty pounds of Luggage, FREE, the same not to exceed ONE THIRD of a TON
measurement.

N. B. Each Passenger is to furnish his own Bed and Bedding.

for Harnden Co
Ch H Saunders

Robert Fulton joined the hoardes of hopeful Argonauts when he purchased this ticket aboard the *Capitol* for the perilous voyage around the Horn.

has been found in considerable quantities. One person brought thirty dollars' worth to New Helvetia, gathered there in a short time. California, no doubt, is rich in mineral wealth; great chances here for scientific capitalists. Gold has been found in almost every part of the country."

On April 26th, the *Californian* said: "From a gentleman just from the gold region, we learn that many new discoveries have very recently been made, and it is fully ascertained that a large extent of the country abounds with that precious mineral. Seven men, with picks and spades, gathered $9,600 within fifteen days. Many persons are settling on the lands with the view of holding pre-emptions, but as yet every person takes the right to gather all he can, without any regard to claims. The largest piece yet found is worth six dollars."

In August, of 1848, the *Californian* reported: "There are now about four thousand white persons, besides a number of Indians, engaged in the mines; and from the fact that no capital is required, they are working in companies, on equal shares, or alone, with their baskets. As to the richness of the mines, were we to set down half the truth, it would be looked upon in other countries as a Sinbad story, or the history of Aladdin's lamp. Many persons have collected in one day the finest grade of gold, from three to eight hundred dollars. . . ."

These sketches are actually navigational aids done by Lieutenant Cadwalader Ringgold. This one is called "Mark for Tongue Shoal."

Sutter's recollections remain a first source of information on just how swiftly the migration to the gold fields exploded and what havoc that explosion wrought. In a recollection dated March 7th, he wrote:

I could say that everybody left me from the Clerk to the Cook. What for great Damages I had to suffer in my tannery which was just doing a profitable and extensive business, and the Vatts was left filled and a quantity of half finished leather was spoiled likewise a large quantity of raw hides collected by the farmers . . . The same thing was in every branch of business which I carried on at the time. I began to harvest my wheat while others was digging and washing Gold, but even the Indians could not be keeped longer . . . and so I had to leave more than 2/3 of my harvest in the fields.

April 28th: "A great many people more went up to the Mountains." May 19th:

The great Rush from San Francisco arrived at the fort, all my friends and acquaintances filled up the houses and the whole fort, I had only a little Indian boy, to make them roasted Ripps etc. as my Cooks left me like every body else . . . The Merchants, Doctors, Lawyers, Sea Captains, Merchants [sic] etc., all came up and did not know what to do, all was in Confusion, all left their wives and families in San Francisco, and those which had none locked their Doors, abandoned their houses, offered them for sale cheap, a few hundred Dollars House & Lot . . . some of these men were just like creazy. Some of the Merchants had been the most prudentest of the whole, visited the Mines and returned immediately and began to do a very profitable business, and soon Vessels came from everywhere with all Kinds of Merchandise.

There was this pertinent entry dated May 25th: "The travelling to the Mines was increasing from day to day, and no more Notice was taken, as the people arrived from South America, Mexico, Sandwich Island, Oregon, etc. . . ."

*The City
Begins*

Brannan was ready for the influx. He had erected a warehouse and provision store. By midyear, Samuel Kyburz rented the fort's central building and established a hotel. As Sutter described it in his later life: "Every little shanty in or around the Fort became a store, a warehouse or a hotel; the whole settlement was a veritable bazaar."

As the waves of migration inundated the settlement, the lord of New Helvetia began to reveal the human weaknesses which were to help bring his ruin. He could not adapt to the new; he vainly sought to keep his empire intact on a business-as-usual basis. Perhaps if he had turned to the new opportunity with the same skills and determination he brought to bear in creating his outpost, he—not Brannan—would have become California's first millionaire.

In these plaguing days Sutter was burdened with still another demand. The Russian-American Fur Company was pressing him to pay his outstanding debt for properties he bought from Fort Ross so many years earlier. The company, hearing of the gold strike, imagined Sutter now must be immensely wealthy.

Frustrated by the life around him, his empire crumbling, his herds decimated by rustlers who peddled the meat to the mining camps at fantastic prices, his fort under assault by Argonauts—Sutter wondered if a younger man might better understand the times, and so he transferred to his son, John Augustus Sutter, Jr., his power of attorney, and retired to Hock Farm. There may have been yet another reason: The Russian-American Fur Company was moving to foreclose his property because of his long-standing debt to the company. The transfer of his property to his son could have put the lands beyond the reach of the Russian-American.

Sutter's son had arrived on the Sacramento scene from Switzerland only a short time before; Mrs. Sutter and the rest of the Sutter children were to arrive in March of 1849 and join him at Hock Farm.

Some years before, Sutter had cut out a roadway between his fort and a stretch of the Sacramento River below its confluence with the American. There he created a port—an Embarcadero—for shipping. In his plan the Embarcadero was to remain a port, nothing more. Trading, he planned, would continue at the fort and, later, at a new village he planned to the south of the port—Sutterville—where trading would be less vulnerable to rising waters.

But just as a watershed in its outpouring will cut its own channel to the seas, so will the growth of a city follow its natural influences.

With the rush of the Argonauts came businessmen. They were aware of an old truth in merchandising: To sell the most, you must put up your shop where the buyer's market is the most promising. And in Sacramento's early

Mrs. John A. Sutter, the former Anna Dubeld, joined Sutter after many years of separation in March of 1849.

This Ringgold sketch is "Entrance to the Sacramento River."

Pt. Cullberg   Montezuma House   Burnett I.   Chain islets.   Montezuma Hills.   Pt. Sacramento

Entrance to the Sacramento River

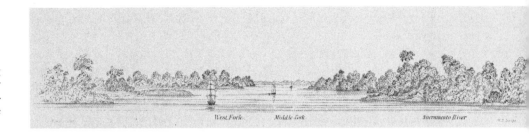

Ringgold sketched "Marks for entering the Sacramento and its Forks at their confluence" (left) and "Mark for entering the second section of the Middle Fork of the Sacramento River."

growth, the buyer's market was to develop at the waterfront—debarkation point for those anxious to get to the gold country.

George McDougal, brother of John McDougal, who would become California's second governor, had arranged with Captain Sutter in 1848 for rights to establish a ferry service on the Sacramento. Soon he converted a ship into the Embarcadero's first store.

Sam Brannan sensed the opportunity, as well. He put up a frame storehouse at Front and J. Hensley and Reading constructed a frame store building at the corner of Front and I streets.

Sutter was outraged with the trading springing up at the Embarcadero. His son, now in command of Sutter's business affairs, did not share his father's sentiments; he saw in the Embarcadero a likely source for real estate development. He engaged Army Captain William H. Warner, assisted by Lieutenant William Tecumseh Sherman, who later was to gain distinction in the Civil War, to survey the Embarcadero and Sutter's other lands for a new Sacramento City, a name for which Brannan later claimed credit.

Almost immediately a trade war developed.

Young Sutter, seeking to negotiate anew the lease his father had given to McDougal for the ferry operation, angered McDougal, who had claimed the exclusive use of the river banks for four hundred yards below a slough which then existed below the confluence. McDougal moved his operations to Sutterville, some three miles south, and—touching off a trade war—offered his goods for sale at cost plus freight.

Not only did this endanger the new Embarcadero trade, it seriously threatened fort profits. Moreover, McDougal offered 80 Sutterville lots free to merchants to establish in Sutterville. Young Sutter countered: He offered 500 lots free to the merchants to settle in Sacramento City. That ended, for all purposes, the business threat from Sutterville, downstream.

Young Sutter engaged Peter H. Burnett, destined to become California's first governor, as agent in the sale of his lots. It was shortly after this that the elder Sutter returned and revoked the power of attorney he had given to his son. However, the potential of this new Sacramento City was evident to Captain Sutter and his later recollections make clear his disappointment. Referring to Sam Brannan, Barton Lee and Pierre Cornwall, Sutter wrote:

They knew that the merchants of Sutterville were their rivals, and it was really jealousy which built the city of Sacramento. This would never have happened, had I not Been snowbound at Coloma. As matters stood, I could do nothing else but

Peter H. Burnett made his fortune selling lots for the Sutters and later became governor of California and a supreme court justice.

agree to everything, even to the name of Sacramento, which my son and Brannan had selected.

At that time the land around the Fort still belonged to me. I had sold a number of lots and given others away gratis. My son had appointed as his agent the future governor, Peter Burnett, who made a fortune much too quickly to suit me. Neither did I like my son's management of the affairs and so I revoked my power of attorney which he held.

John Sutter, Jr., departed for Mexico, where he lived a prosperous life. His father reluctantly accepted the reality of a city by the Embarcadero and tried to make the most of the situation. The fortunes of the man were to become dimmer and dimmer, but those of the city were to grow brighter and brighter.

After Hensley & Reading had erected their store building, a Mr. Ingersoll put up a structure, half canvas and half frame, between J and K on Front, and a Mr. Stewart opened a tavern, in canvas, between I and J on the riverbank. Then came the Brannan storehouse, succeeded by another built by Priest, Lee & Co. on the corner of J and 2nd.

However, Sacramento's population, including fort and city, still was not much more than 150 in April 1849. While the city was doing a brisk business outfitting Argonauts, the population explosion was to come in midsummer.

Even then, trading was yielding vast profits. In San Francisco, flour was selling for $16 per hundredweight; cattle at $30 a head. Sacramento was selling flour at $35 a hundredweight; cattle at $70 a head.

A tin of oysters was bringing $12. Cabin passage on riverboats cost $30, San Francisco to Sacramento. Hammers were priced at $8 to $10, picks at $20. Freight on goods came to $50 a ton, and a dollar a foot on logs. A small schooner for river trading was bringing $20,000. Clerks in stores were making $500 a month—when they could be kept.

Prices and the Crowds

This Ringgold sketch of Sacramento City is more work of art than navigational aid, but does warn of a very active port.

CALIFORNIA AND THE GOLD DIGGINGS.   LIFE ON THE SACRAMENTO.

A New York publication called the *Pictorial Jonathan* gives us this whimsical look at life during the Gold Rush—hectic, crowded.

A truly immense trade was springing up between Sacramento and the mines. Dr. John F. Morse, renowned in early Sacramento history and one of its most faithful chroniclers, wrote: "Miners came to town freighted with bags of gold, which they stored away as indifferently as they did their hats and boots."

By May 1, 1849, there were some 30 buildings of the crudest variety being used for stores and warehouses. The destination of the Argonauts: the American, the Bear, the Yuba and the Feather Rivers, and the Sierra highlands. Sacramento was outfitter for all.

Sam Brannan had added to his holdings on the Embarcadero by erecting another store. His name appears too with the construction of the first hotel. With John S. Fowler, Brannan acquired lumber from Sutter's idle grist mill at Brighton and built the two-story Hotel de France on Front Street north of J. A three-story structure built, so it is said, at a cost of $100,000, rose shortly afterward next door: the City Hotel.

So massive was the immigration that hundreds were forced to sleep and camp in the open. Soon the Embarcadero began to resemble a forest of masts—for what ship captain could hold a crew with the diggings so close?

But a wayside for the goldseeker must offer more than picks and pans and bedrolls. Inevitable to such settlements was the saloon, the gambling hall.

In the first months of the influx, the new city was surprisingly free of those temptations. The only place one could wet the lip was at Sutter's Fort. There was little of what historians call "loose morality." This was true even though there were, as yet, virtually no legal restraints—except the certainty of frontier justice at the end of a rope.

By the summer of 1849, however, a little "loose morality" came to the city. The first of the Argonaut playpens of any reputation, the Stinking Tent arose, a makeshift gaming emporium composed of a few poles stuck in the ground and covered with wind-sail. It was operated by James Lee between 2nd and 3rd on J. If one is mildly curious about why it came to be called the Stinking Tent, the downwind side would explain it quickly.

Z. Hubbard's Round Tent followed. It had more class, was less offensive both to the eye and the nostril. Built also of canvas, on J between Front and 2nd, and linked to the Eagle Theater, it covered some 50 feet in diameter and offered such diversions as music, a handsomely decorated bar and a picture gallery of girls in the half together and the all together. Morse recalls it as offering "every species of gambling in its most seductive aspect." It would be criminal to neglect this quote, also by Morse:

"The toilers of the country, including traders, mechanics and speculators, lawyers, doctors, and some apostate ministers, concentrated at this gambling focus, like insects around a lighted candle at night: and like insects, seldom left the delusive glare until scorched and consumed by the fires of destruction."

Small wonder that other emporiums would follow, and profit immensely, with hundred dollar ante games not uncommon. The Gem at J and 2nd; the Humboldt, the Mansion, the Empire, Lee's Exchange, Diana, the El Dorado. One writer said of the Argonaut and that period: "They came in droves from the Sierra diggings, and Here they gambled new-mined dust. And then wrote home, again to say: 'No money, wife—next time, perhaps, the pickings have been slim.'"

Dr. John F. Morse treated cholera victims in 1850, was an early editor of the *Union*, and wrote the city's first history in 1853.

But the migrant was more concerned about the creature comforts than he was with the town's morals. The autobiography of Stephen C. Massett reveals this. He tells of arriving in 1849 after a six-day trip upstream, of taking a bath in the river at "even-tide," and of getting lodging at the still-incomplete City Hotel. He wrote:

I think mine was the corner "bunk". . . The heat was insufferable, mosquitoes were buzzing about, and with their slow though sure attendants, fleas and bed-bugs came in myriads to greet and congratulate me on my arrival. Scratching and itching, itching and scratching, kept me pretty well awake all night; and then the stifled smell —the noise inside and out—the swearing and snoring of the occupants, the barking of dogs, the leaving of numberless trains of mules and donkeys outside, the cries of children, rended the scene perfect pandemonium—and to crown the whole, just as I had managed from sheer exhaustion to drop off into a doze, I felt a heavy bump come up against the slender board that screened me from the street—when to my astonishment the head of a big ox presented itself, and with its cold and moist snout commenced rubbing against my knees!

As for the rampant land speculation he found, he wrote:

A man would buy a tract of land or a "rancho" for perhaps $1,000 or so—he would have it staked out or cut up into "lots," call it a city—get some draughtsmen to make beautiful and gaudy maps thereof, insist that it was either the "head of navigation" or the nearest route to the best diggings—unsurpassed for agricultural purposes, and so on. One instance I well remember—the place was called "Butte City," I believe the original cost was $1,000. I was directed to sell as many lots as I possibly could at that figure per lot, and I think the embryo city yielded the fortunate speculator about $20,000—the reader need not be informed that the place was then, is now, and ever will be, a barren waste—world without end—amen!

It is a law of life that when the gambler and the speculator come, the preacher is not far behind.

There is some confusion in early history on who preached the first sermon. Some say the Rev. Mr. Woodbridge, and others say, J. W. Douglas. The account claiming the Rev. Mr. Woodbridge was the first to bring the Book to the Argonauts, says he preached in the "open air to about sixty persons," but made "only one effort." It does not elaborate, and leaves, instead, the intriguing question: did he conclude the Sacramento sinner was beyond redemption, or did he have other fires to burn elsewhere?

Regardless, Methodist-Episcopalian Pastor W. Grove Deal is credited with establishing the first regular and continuing services in May, 1849—largely nondenominational and addressed by other pastors, such as the Rev. Mr. Cook, a Baptist clergyman who operated a boarding house on I Street.

Perhaps the most distinctive of the early-day pastors to attempt to bring God to the spiritual wilderness of a young city was the Rev. J. A. Benton who arrived from Connecticut in July, 1849. The biographer, Dr. Morse, said of him: "He was a seven-days' advocate of the Christian religion. He was around among and one of the people; his brow was seldom clouded with intolerant observation and his tongue was not too bitterly charged with denunciation; hence, he wielded a moral influence outside the immediate sphere of church worshippers. . . ."

There is this excerpt from one of his sermons which tells us something about the man and his time, and the Argonaut.

Ah, if such as dwell far away, if parents and guardians, if wives and children, if brothers, sisters, and those other loving ones, should hear concerning your habits of drinking, your revels, and your debauches, would they believe? If they heard that your evenings were passed in the saloon, and that all the proceeds of your labor and the profits of your business were swept into the coffers of gamesters, deceptive, deft and adroit, could they receive it as true? If they should be made to know, as we too well know, your indifferences, your delinquencies, your sensualities, your gross in-

William Grove Deal (above) is credited with establishing the first regular and continuing religious services in Sacramento in May of 1849. J. A. Benton started in July of that year and was a powerful figure for years.

fidelities, what havoc would there be of human happiness, human hopes, human hearts: How would love slighted and trust betrayed turn to indignation and abhorrence, which years could scarce abate? Beware, yet whose feet are in these paths of death, lest, while ye destroy yourselves, ye dash many another's cup with bitterness, and bring down grey hairs with sorrow to the grave!

If this were the "gentle" admonition suggested by Dr. Morse in his biography, what damnation must the other pastors have evoked upon the gaming Argonaut?

Dr. Benton was to organize the large First Church of Christ in September, 1849. Its members pointedly omitted the designation Congregational, which they were, and thereby attracted huge congregations by not emphasizing denomination. Grove's Protestant Episcopal Church was slightly earlier in establishing its congregation, organizing in a blacksmith shop on 3rd Street in August, 1849. The Presbyterians found sufficient comfort in Benton's church to delay the founding of their own church until 1856.

By the end of 1849, there were no less than four Protestant denominations.

Artist George V. Cooper, in yet another drawing for *California Illustrated*, provided this view of the City of Tents in 1849.

COOPER DEL   ON STONE BY J. CAMERON

ENCAMPMENT AT SAC CITY, NOV. 1849.

The route to the mines was a clogged one,
as shown by George V. Cooper, and the mobility was
supplied by everything from foot to ox.

Charles Nahl, one of the busiest and most
widely reproduced artists of California scenes, had this
impression of wayside scenes in Wide West,
a San Francisco pictorial newspaper.

CALIFORNIA

Its Past History
ITS PRESENT POSITION
ITS FUTURE PROSPECTS

SCENE ON A BRANCH OF THE SACRAMENTO.

London.
Printed for the Booksellers.
1850.

A London edition used this setting for its title page in 1850. Books on the nature of California were in great demand, and while many were of doubtful accuracy, there were some of quality and beauty.

By the end of 1849, the Argonauts were greeted by hotels, businesses, and a canvas gaming palace, as well as California's first theater: The Eagle. William McIlvaine created this view of Front Street.

Grass Valley had a population of 4,000 in 1851 when this lithograph was made of the Grass Valley Quartz Mining Company. The information with this print gives great detail about the mill, including its capacity of 30 to 40 tons of ore in 24 hours, producing up to 180 ounces of gold.

The Roman Catholics became represented in August of 1850 with the arrival of Rev. Augustine P. Anderson from New Jersey. Fire, wind, and flood frustrated their efforts to erect a lasting church until 1854 when Archbishop Alemany laid the cornerstone for the brick St. Rose of Lima at 7th and K, on land deeded to the church in 1850 by Peter Burnett. And Jewish pioneers were to organize their first synagogue when the Hebrew Benevolent Society established the Congregation B'Nai Israel, in 1861, but nine years earlier the Congregation Children of Israel (later B'nai Israel) purchased the Methodist Episcopal Church on the east side of 7th between L and M streets, dedicating it as Sacramento's first synagogue; the date: June 4, 1852.

Nor does a community, wherever it has promise of growth, exist long without a newspaper. In the case of Sacramento, it was Edward C. Kemble who brought the written word to the city.

Kemble was one of the original proprietors of the *Alta California* in San Francisco. He sensed Sacramento's opportunity and in the spring of 1849 took a box full of old type, a few quires of paper, a press, stowed them on board a launch, and set out for Sutter's Embarcadero. It took him eight days to make the passage.

Lieutenant Gould Buffum in an account of his meeting with Kemble said

The Newspaper Arrives

61

he was "sick with what everybody in the vicinity of Sacramento then expected to have a touch of, upon his arrival—that interesting disease, fever and ague. He was weak, pale and thin, but filled with an enthusiastic determination to succeed, and establish on a firm basis, a newspaper."

Establishing his shop at Sutter's Fort—not the Embarcadero—Kemble came out with his first issue on April 28, 1849, and called it the *Placer Times*.

Kemble remained in Sacramento only until June, however, when increasing illness forced him to return to San Francisco. T. P. PerLee and Co. operated the *Times* for a while and then J. H. Giles, an agent for the owners of the San Francisco-based *Alta California* and once a writer for Horace Greely's New York *Tribune*.

Few imagined then that Sacramento would come to be known, in the years which followed, as the "graveyard of newspapers." From 1849 to 1858 between 50 and 60 newspapers were founded, and of these all but two perished: the *Sacramento Union* established in 1851, and the *Sacramento Bee*, in 1857.

"This delightful place…"

What was the city like in those early, building years? Say 1850? After the migration to the gold fields had reached its peak, the city was beginning to take on some dimension, a government was being formed, and Sacramento was taking on a more live-in than travel-through appearance.

There is this account, somewhat romantic but revealing, which appeared over the initials F. M. in the San Francisco *California Courier*, in 1850, quoted in part:

I have told you I had very moderate expectations of Sacramento. You can imagine my surprise at seeing a great and thriving city, with a broad levee, where vessels of considerable burthen could discharge their cargoes at once, without any heed of the caprice of wind and tide. . . . Immense trees covered, with their graceful shade, this scene of busy industry; for here vast quantities of goods were landing, and crowds of merchants, traders and laborers were actively employed in the various pursuits of business. . . . Here were water carts constantly at work, with the characteristic inscription "Down with the dust;" the dust of Ophir!. . . . Omnibuses were running from point to point. "Time Is Money!". . . . [You are] treated with that kind consideration which makes you forget you are a stranger in a strange land. But this is a general feature of the place; the people all seem to partake the generous character of the climate. If the soil is rich in untold wealth, the hearts of the people who inhabit it seem to have acquired, in equal profusion, those fine mineral qualities, without which all this prosperity would be a curse. . . . They have an Operahouse, Theatre and Circus so well patronized as to prove that gain is not an all absorbing pursuit; but that amusement and relaxation are wisely intermingled in the common business of life . . . We crossed the river in a steam ferry . . . Think of that!. . . . Here, too, are evidences of domestic comfort. Pretty cottages, each surrounded with its own garden, show that families are established here, and have made homes for themselves in this beautiful climate. . . . The water is sweet and clear. . . . One thing surprised me very much. I visited a plantation just across the river from Sacramento and saw melons, tomatoes, corn, potatoes etc. growing as luxuriantly without irrigation, as on the most cultivated lands. . . . You may imagine it was with some regret I left this delightful place, bearing with me a most grateful recollection of the generous

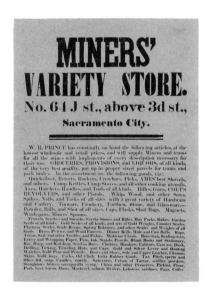

This broadside for the Miners' Variety Store includes an extensive list of just about everything Mr. Prince had "constantly on hand."

Sutter's retreat, after he turned his business affairs over to his son, was Hock Farm on the Feather River. John Bidwell had helped Sutter lay it out many years earlier.

hospitality with which I had been entertained, and desiring and resolving very soon again to visit the pleasant little "village" of Sacramento.

Allow for the literary excesses, for overstatement, for the fact F. M. found so much more than he/she expected; but by this time in its life, 1850, Sacramento had reached the home-and-garden stage of family life; it had public transportation by the river, for "time is money"; it had steam-operated ferries; settlers still had not stripped the land of trees; merchants and tradesmen were profiting from brisk business; water carts sought to still the dust of the streets; the water was sweet, pure, and the soil was rich. It was a city coming into its own.

A Time of Challenge

Chapter Four

BY THE SPRING OF 1849, it was becoming apparent that the new city would have to establish some kind of government. Sacramento was flourishing. There was the certainty the migration of miners had barely begun. And while there had been no unruliness—remarkable in the wake of the crowds —it was becoming obvious that some instrument for order would have to be established. And somehow the city's business would have to be managed.

Proceeding to the first priority, the city elected a board of commissioners. The commission met under an oak tree near the riverfront at the foot of what is now I Street, and there drew up boundaries for the new city and proceeded to draft a framework for government.

They thought big. The board claimed for Sacramento City all lands in the "district embraced between the Sacramento River, the Sierra Nevada, and the Cosumnes," and all lands north and south through the great length of the Sacramento Basin—or roughly one-fourth of what today is California.

It would be a paper empire, but it was symbolic of the appetite possessed by the men organizing the government, and their commitment to the new adventure: Samuel Brannan, Jacob R. Snyder, Peter Slater, Samuel J. Hensley, James King, Henry Cheever, Morton M. McCarver, John McDougal, Barton Lee. And others: A. P. Petit, William Carpenter, John Fowler, Charles Southard, all members of the original board.

The months passed. Still Sacramento had no formal government. Only the boundary had been drawn and an alcalde created. Then in July, 1849, the community elected its first council in a meeting of the townspeople in the St. Louis Exchange; there they drafted a charter and established committees to act on key community problems.

What was the city like in this stage of its growth? Building was going up rapidly on J, on Front, on K. The riverfront was a veritable bazaar. Storage was in very short supply.

Lumber was also in critical supply: It was bringing up to $1 a board foot.

Though from this detail it would appear that the flood waters were not deep, they did ruin whatever was in first floors and in every tent not on high ground.

A detail from the Casselear and Bainbridge lithograph shows what the young Sacramento City sustained and overcame in its early years before it was able to resist fire and flood.

65

Freight dealers were making a small fortune, getting $50 a hundredweight in shipments from Sacramento to the foothill diggings. Bread was bringing 50c a loaf; butter, $3 a pound. Milk, $1 a quart. Dried apples, $2 a pound. Lodging, without board, was going at $50 a week, and more. A glass of liquor cost $1; a cigar 50c.

Transport on the river, of course, was at a premium. The steamboat *Sacramento* was being built on the riverfront, a mile above the city, and was to be launched in September, 1849. Some 10 steamboats were to be in operation on the river before the year's end, including the *Senator*, the *Enterprise*, the *Eclipse*. Riverboat cabins were going for $30, San Francisco to Sacramento. One dredge carried bricks at a dollar each and lumber at $150 per thousand board feet.

The time had come, as well, for the establishment of a post office; so critical was the building shortage that the post office was created aboard the bark *Whiton* in July, 1849. Only weeks earlier the *Whiton* had astonished Sacramentans by sailing from San Francisco to Sacramento in just 72 hours in spite of her relatively large burden, 241 tons, and her deep draw, 9½ feet. Henry E. Robinson, a merchant, was named postmaster. Shortly the post office was moved from the *Whiton* to Robinson's store on J between Front and 2nd. Federal records note that an authorized post office was granted permanently on November 8, 1849.

The population explosion, while centering in the city, was not exclusive to Sacramento. The pressures were being felt throughout the north state; military government no longer sufficed.

General Bennett Riley, who had been named civil governor, was persuaded to call for an election of delegates to a convention in Monterey at which a state constitution was proposed. The Sacramento District sent eight delegates. The city representatives were Jacob R. Snyder, and M. M. McCarver. Three delegates were listed as being from Sutter, or what was more commonly known as Sutterville. They were Lansford W. Hastings, John McDougal, and John Augustus Sutter. Winfield Sherwood was the delegate from Mormon Island, E. O. Crosby from Vernon, and W. E. Shannon from Coloma, at that time a part of the Sacramento District. The constitution was ratified by the voters overwhelmingly in November. And Burnett, who had served as John Sutter Jr.'s chief representative in the disposition of the senior Sutter's lands in the city, was elected the state's first governor.

Sacramento City had somewhat more difficulty in adopting its charter for government. The gambling houses rallied successfully to defeat the first proposal offered in September, 1849: A government-less Sacramento suited the gamblers' interest with the only jurisdiction an alcalde's court. The charter lost by 146 votes.

Later in the fall, townspeople beat down the gambling influence, adopting the charter—calling for the establishment of a government, a council, and legal authority and courts—by a 296-vote margin.

On February 27, 1850, Sacramento City officially was granted its charter by the first California Legislature; days earlier, the legislature had created county government when it divided the state into county units. Statehood had

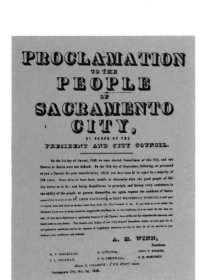

This 1849 proclamation by the city councilmen asked for citizens to suggest a new charter for the one rejected by voters.

not been granted; that was to come months later. The next legislature granted a request to drop the word "City" from the name and Sacramento it has been ever since.

Even in the exhilarating climate of Gold Rush Sacramento, man did not live by bread alone, or by gold, either. As always, he made art, too. Up in the Mother Lode, in 1849, an artist named George V. Cooper was drawing the sketches of mining life that were to gain fame later in a book, published in New York, called *California Illustrated*. Down on the Sacramento River, a young fellow from Massachusetts named George Holbrook Baker drew the busy Embarcadero and the ships at anchor there, the first of many such drawings

The Theater Arts

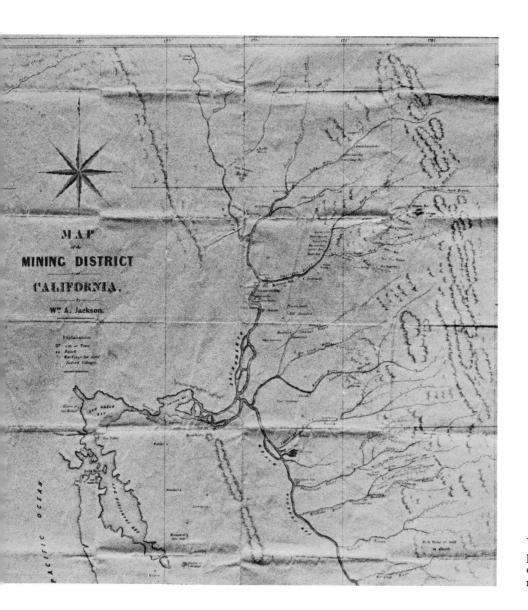

William A. Jackson produced this tissue paper map of the mining district, which concentrated on the early activity in the north.

Though Sacramento began with a few buildings on Front between I and J in 1848, by 1850 substantial buildings such as these appeared on Front between N and O.

that became engravings which showed the world what the Gold Rush was like.

Men sang, of course, and could buy broadsides on the street with the words to "Poor Old Horse, Let Him Die," "My Poor Dog Tray," and "The Pioneer Stage Driver," the last with a picture of the composer, Charley Rhoades. Charley came to California literally with a banjo on his knee—they say he introduced the instrument to the state—in 1849 at the age of 18 and stayed for 20 years. His "The Days of '49" has been described as the unofficial state song of the pioneers.

But by far a more significant single artistic event of those first years was the opening of the first theater built in California, the Eagle, on the Sacramento Embarcadero on October 18, 1849.

There had already been a few dramatic performances elsewhere, notably those given by the men of Stevenson's regiment in Monterey, but they were staged in improvised surroundings. The Eagle was a real theater, and the company which took up residence there in October was professional. (It was this performance which the owners regarded as the opening of the Eagle, although the Stockton Minstrels had played there September 25 and 27.)

Professional theater began in California with a bandit, a knight, and a damsel in distress: With *The Bandit Chief; or The Spectre of the Forest*, which shared a double bill with a comedy by John Howard Payne called *Love in Humble Life*. The players were a company assembled by Charles Price, who thus became California's first actor-manager. Among the leading players were Mr. and Mrs. Henry Ray, newly arrived from New Zealand. They were greeted opening night by what the local *Placer Times* described as "a full, and we may add, fashionable house, for the 'dress circle' was graced by quite a number of fine looking well-costumed ladies, the sight of whom was somewhat revivifying."

The playhouse itself was an impressive enterprise, even by the high-priced standards of the day. It cost about $75,000. The builder was Z. Hubbard, reputed to be one of a triumvirate which built the first theater in Texas.

The Eagle was a wooden frame building with canvas sides, designed to seat about 400 within an area of about 30 by 95 feet. Lumber for the frame cost between $600 and $700 per thousand feet; canvas came at $1 a yard; the carpenters earned $50 a day and the man who painted the front curtain and the backdrops got $50 a day.

One entrance was through the Round Tent, a gambling "hell" and saloon immediately adjacent, but the balcony could also be reached by way of a ladder outside the theater, shielded by a canvas for the benefit of the ladies.

Fortunately for posterity, that first performance was attended by two distinguished reporters: Bayard Taylor, a world-traveled author who had been sent west by Horance Greeley's New York *Tribune* to write about the Gold Rush, and Stephen Massett, a remarkable combination of songwriter, singer, actor, entrepreneur, and rolling stone who had arrived in San Francisco from his native London only two months before.

"It had been raining hard and blowing a gale of wind all day," Massett later wrote, "and the strength and durability of the building had been sorely tried: however, as the hour drew near for the opening of the doors, crowds of anxious miners thronged the entrance, and despite the winds and torrents of rain, the place was immediately filled."

And here is Taylor, in his book called *El Dorado*:

The spectators are dressed in heavy overcoats and felt hats, with boots reaching to the knees. . . . The sides and roof of the theatre are canvas, which when wet, effectually prevents ventilation, and renders the atmosphere hot and stifling. The drop-curtain, which is down at present, exhibits a glaring landscape, with dark-brown trees in the foreground, and lilac-colored mountains against a yellow sky.

The overture commences; the orchestra is composed only of five members, under the direction of an Italian, and performs with tolerable correctness. The piece for the night is "The Spectre Of The Forest" in which the celebrated actress, Mrs. Ray, "of the Royal Theatre, New Zealand," will appear. The bell rings; the curtain rolls up; and we look upon a forest scene, in the midst of which appears Hildebrand, the robber, in a sky-blue mantle. The foliage of the forest is of dark-red color, which makes a great impression on the spectators and prepares them for the bloody scenes that are to follow. The other characters are a brave knight in a purple dress, with his servant in scarlet; they are about to storm the robbers' hold and carry off a captive maiden. Several acts are filled with the usual amount of fighting and terrible speeches; but the interest of the play is carried to an awful height by the appearance of two spectres, clad in mutilated tent-covers, and holding spermaceti candles in their hands. At this juncture Mrs. Ray rushes in and throws herself into an attitude in the middle of the stage: why she does it, no one can tell. This movement, which she repeats several times in the course of the first three acts, has no connection with the tragedy; it is evidently introduced for the purpose of showing the audience that there is, actually, a female performer. The miners, to whom the sight of a woman is not a frequent occurrence, are delighted with these passages and applaud vehemently.

In the closing scenes, where Hildebrand entreats the heroine to beome his bride, Mrs. Ray shone in all her glory. "No!" said she, "I'd rather take a basilisk and wrap

During the spring of 1850, John Wood-house Audubon, a descendant of the famed naturalist-painter, visited Sacramento City. The younger Audubon was a painter too, and left an impressive view of the tree-filled village.

its cold fangs around me, than be clasped in the hembraces of an 'artless robber." Then changing her tone to that of entreaty, she calls upon the knight in purple, whom she declares to be "me 'ope—me only 'ope!" We will not stay to hear the songs and duetts which follow; the tragedy has been a sufficient infliction.

Expenses were high at the Eagle and the weather was often rough; floods sometimes covered the benches on the lower floor, and the miners had fun pushing each other into the water. Within a month the theater closed, but a few days later—November 17—it opened again with a new manager, a Mr.

Atwater, who had played Hildebrand in *The Bandit Chief*. In the weeks that followed, a variety of plays typical of the time was offered: *Box and Cox*, *Douglas*, *Beacon of Death*, *Charles II*, and others, including a revival of *The Bandit Chief*.

"We had a pretty good company, and were playing to good business," John H. McCabe, a member of the troupe who went on to a long career in California theater, recalled later. "Money was plentiful and everybody spent it freely."

But then came the great flood of early January, 1850: "Well, it commenced to rain, and it kept on raining . . . until the entire place was under water, and the

Joseph Andrew Rowe, "the celebrated equestrian and domesticator of the horse," had his own Sacramento pavillion, built by Sam Brannan.

71

flood drove us out. We left everything in the way of scenery, fixtures and properties right there, and brought with us to San Francisco our wearing apparel and the very incomplete stage wardrobe we possessed."

That was the end of the Eagle, but it was only the end of a brave beginning. Within a few months new theaters were opening in town, including a relocated, rebuilt version of the Eagle called the Tehama. The lively, colorful parade of actors, dancers, minstrel men, circus riders, burlesque queens, child prodigies and comedians was to make Sacramento a theater center second to none in the state.

Test by Flood

The flood which wiped out the Eagle also wiped out a great number of other businesses.

It descended with unexpected suddenness. In the evening of January 8 came a violent storm out of the south. The ground, already saturated with run-offs from heavy storms in December and the first week in January, could absorb no more. Both the Sacramento and the American crested, and great walls of water washed onto the floor of the young city—facing, in that moment, its first test with the elements.

The diary of Dr. John Morse, distinguished physician and civic leader in the building years, serves best to recreate the panic and the mood of the city. It follows, in part:

Everyone was inclined to believe the ridiculous and false assurance of safety, which could scarcely be extinguished when the city was actually under water. Hence when the water began to rush in and overwhelm the place, there was no adequate means of escape for life and property; and consequently some were drowned in their beds, and many died in consequences of the terrible exposures to which they were subjected. The few boats belonging to the shipping were brought into requisition in gathering up the women, children and invalids that were scattered about in tents in remote, low places, and were found standing upon beds and boxes, in water a foot deep, and which was still rising with perilous rapidity. Sick men, utterly helpless, were found floating about on cots, and, in the enfeebled tone of dissolution, were crying for help.

Hundreds of thousands of dollars worth of merchandise piled on the Embarcadero was swept away. One man—he was called the Dutchman—kept his gold in a belly bank, or money belt as it is more politely termed. He perished when a small boat sank; he could not support both his gold and himself, and apparently chose to go down with his poke.

Owners of small boats made fortunes. A whaleboat brought $30 an hour for hire; it would sell, in that hour of crisis, for $1,000. The property loss was staggering, including provisions swept away in the first assault of the waters. The flood victims took any high rise of ground they could find and made makeshift tents. The more provident left in the minutes of the first warning, and found higher ground beyond, to the east.

The deluge ended, the sky cleared, and by January 18 most of the city had dug out of the debris, counted its losses, and returned to the task of reconstruction. By February, trading had resumed with the mines. After this respite, and just as Sacramento imagined the danger was over, heavy rains and melting snows combined in March to bring a new overflow—an overflow which might have been the January inundation all over again had it not been for Hardin Bigelow.

After the January flood, Bigelow gave leadership in building minimal levees, damming up the sloughs and all low ground. Driving a small group of levee tenders to—and beyond—their limits, he directed flood control emergency measures which saved the city. So popular was Bigelow that one month later he was elected mayor—Sacramento's first.

With its initial inundation, Sacramento courted no further illusions. The Indians had talked of a great flood which had struck the bottomland country some 45 years earlier, and a second flood which had inundated the valley some 25 years earlier; but both came before the white man's settlement. The city knew it would have to turn to the task of erecting levees; the conviction had emerged as a hard fact of life.

Three months after the flood, Sacramento faced the first of what would be many tests by fire. On April 4, fire broke out on Front between J and K streets; shortly, eight to ten buildings were consumed.

The way with which the pioneer met the test by fire, as well as by flood, was best illustrated perhaps by the story of one merchant wiped out in the April fire. The *Placer Times* recorded: "Messers. Hoope & L'Amoureux, who lost their entire stock of Spring goods, will open Monday at the same old stand."

In November, a second fire is recorded. This one destroyed four hotels—the New York, the Eagle, the St. Francis and the Galena. It also took out an establishment with the romantic name Home of the Badger and several provision stores. The total damage: about $45,000.

These fires, minor in comparison to several which would follow in the next years, were enough to alert Sacramento to the need for more careful protection, and inspired the establishment of volunteer fire companies which served the city not only as defense against fire but as organizations around which to rally socially.

In fact, Sacramento was to become the first city in the state to organize a volunteer fire fighting unit, The Mutual Hook and Ladder Company. In the decade which followed, 13 such companies were to be organized.

The constant threat of fire produced another familiar sight: the use of iron shutters over windows. They made buildings less susceptible to draft, and consequently to fire. So effective were they that builders in the Gold Country adopted the use of iron shutters in their construction. Some remain today in the Gold Country as well as in Sacramento, a testament to the time and age of the building years.

Sacramento was exceptionally vulnerable, however.

Before the rash of fires which were to engulf Sacramento, San Francisco twice was all but wiped out and virtually all of the pioneer settlements, with their board and canvas buildings and their lack of protection, were prey to fire, and most were burned in whole or in part.

And by Fire

Growth and Unrest

By April of 1850, Sacramento County held its first election even though the state constitution, authorizing the county unit and establishing the authority for election, still had not been sanctioned by the federal government.

E. J. Willis was elected county judge. Joseph McKinney, a young gambling hall operator, was named sheriff. John H. McKune was elected county attorney.

The processes for order had been created.

There are charming little anecdotes of the burgeoning years which make for delightful reminiscing:

—So-called land sharks were not coddled. In 1849, a William Muldrow was sentenced to receive twelve lashes across his bare back, and the order of the court was that the last was to be well laid on. Muldrow was given an alternative: he could escape the whip if he would leave town within twelve hours. He did.

—Signs gracing the city reflected the romance of the nineteenth century lilt in the written word. One read: "Tip top accommodations for man and beast." Another: "Rest for the weary and storage for trunks." A third: "Come in the inn and take a bite." A restaurant got right down to cases in its advertising, saying: "Eating is done here."

—The *Alta California* listed the daily stages leaving Sacramento: Six to Marysville, two to Coloma and one each to Nevada City, Placerville, Auburn, Stockton and Drytown, and Jackson. The Sacramento-Marysville run alone was accommodating some 70 passengers each day; and fares, at their peak, reached $1 a mile.

—If any one incident reveals the gold craze which consumed the early city, there was the day in 1850—on January 18—when an unidentified miner discovered some shiny flakes at the foot of J Street during the flood. The word got around: Shortly miners were sloshing, ankle deep, looking for "color." The *Placer Times* reported: "There have been flakes of gold found in our streets within the few days past and we saw a gentleman yesterday who had washed out quite a pile on the banks of the Sacramento." Less excited observers were skeptical. They reasoned, and probably quite correctly, the flakes apparently had been deposited by muddy flood waters pouring down the Yuba, American, and Sacramento.

—The man who wanted public office more desperately than any in Sacramento's early history—perhaps in all of its history—was a Colonel Joseph Grant, who came to the gold country by way of the Horn to make his fortune and name. Running for mayor in 1850, Grant faced three opponents and, literally stumping on a whisky keg in front of waterfront saloons, he averaged some 30 speeches a day. And when each was finished, he would call for a round of drinks for all who had listened. What that bit of frontier electioneering may have cost him is mercifully lost in history, but the report was he did draw good crowds. Grant may have had a faithful following, saloon to saloon. But when election time came, his following failed him. He lost. So he departed, sailing upriver where he was one of the founders of the town of Nicolaus and where he made enough money selling lots of $100 to $800 each to finance an election campaign there. And there he got himself elected mayor, by a slim margin.

Demas Strong was elected to the city council in March, 1850, and became acting mayor when Hardin Bigelow was wounded in the Squatters Riot.

—So in demand was permanent housing in the young city that Sacramento County had to rent the bark *Strafford* for jail quarters in 1850. The time came when her owners wished to put again to sea so the county shopped around and found another ship it turned into a jail—the *La Grange*—which survived, in that use, until the flood of 1862 when it sank.

—Enterprise was not restricted to the gold fields. Good drinking water was in short supply when William E. Henry arrived on the scene in 1850. He attempted to turn water into gold—something the alchemists never could quite bring off—by filling buckets of water from the river with a pump and selling water door to door. He might have made his fortune in the effort had not another enterprising, newly arrived Sacramentan cut into his business by pumping water, and selling it door to door, from the old Sutter Slough.

—The theory that the Sacramento Valley once may have been a lake or ocean bed was proposed almost from the beginning. In a report to Secretary of State John Clayton in 1850, Government Agent Thomas Butler King wrote: "The great valley of the Sacramento and San Joaquin has evidently been, at some remote period, the bed of a lake; and those rivers which drain it, present the appearance of having cut their channels through the alluvial deposit after it had been formed."

—And as for the soil, King wrote: "The soil is very rich, and, with a proper system of drainage and embankment, would, undoubtedly, be capable of producing any crop, except sugarcane, now cultivated in the Atlantic states. There are many beautiful valleys and rich hillsides among the foothills of the Sierra Nevada which when the profits of labor in mining shall be reduced as to cause its application to agriculture, will probably support a large population."

Which, of course, is exactly what happened. Sutter had been right: the real future of this rich valley was not gold; its destiny was the land.

The *La Grange* served as the city's jail for over a dozen years before she sank in the flood of 1862.

The story comes, now, to one of the most dramatic episodes in the young city's history: The Squatters Riot. It involved one of the oldest of quarrels between men: the right to land. And the issue was not confined exclusively to the region of Sacramento.

History differs in its interpretation of events leading to the confrontation

The Squatters Riot

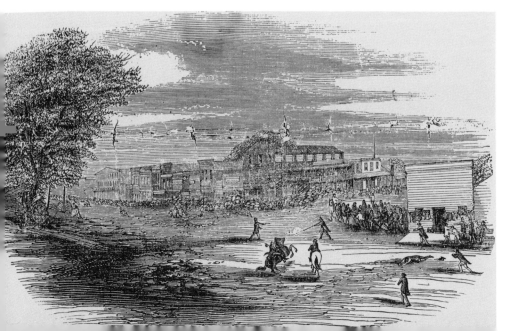

This dramatic woodcut shows the Squatters Riot confrontation at 4th and J Streets when several were killed and wounded, including the mayor and tax assessor.

between the vested and the divested—or to put it more directly, between those who held title to the land in the new city and those who questioned the moral, even legal, right to such title. It is an issue which can be scanned through as many mirrors as one might wish to hold to that history.

In the view of some, the squatters had a perfect right to the land. These held the land was frontier, that the original titles were in legal question, and therefore that the land should be available for the taking. The other view was that the titles were valid, that right to the property was clearly established and that, therefore, the squatters had neither the moral nor the legal claim to take land by the simple right of possession.

This work shall be content to leave the question to more definitive examination. Suffice it, for this purpose, to recreate the issue, as the pioneers lived it.

To appreciate the dimension of the problem statewide, consider this brief summary by Paul W. Gates in an article, "California's Embattled Settlers," published in the *California Historical Society Quarterly* in June, 1962:

Land seekers arriving in California in 1848—and after the first years of the gold rush most immigrants wanted land—found a most confused complex of seemingly insoluble problems facing them. . . . From San Diego to Shasta, in the coastal valleys, in the Sacramento and San Joaquin valleys, and in the Bay region there were some 800 private claims that called for between thirteen million and fourteen million acres of land. A heritage from the Spanish-Mexican period . . . mostly they ranged in size from one to eleven leagues of 4,426 acres to the league. . . . More than half of the eight hundred claims were based on grants made in the years just prior to American control.

The crux of the quarrel: The settler could not concede the right of 800 claims to some 14 million acres of land.

The settlers who poured into Sacramento, most in search of gold but others in search of land, found no fences, no markings, no stipulated boundaries. And so they settled on the land—claiming it out of the old frontier tradition of the right of pre-emption, right of occupancy. They refused to recognize the right of one man, Sutter, to 22 leagues of land. And they refused to recognize the land titles of tracts bought up cheaply by speculators, and then offered at prohibitive prices.

There were two other objections on the part of the settlers to the Sutter grant. Sutter claimed lands north of latitude 38 degrees, 41 minutes, 32 seconds. Colonel John Frémont, who was dispatched some years earlier by President Van Buren to survey the Western country, had different readings, however. He gave a latitude of 38 degrees, 34 minutes, 42 seconds for Sacramento. This placed Sacramento several miles south of Sutter's Mexican grant, they claimed, and they asked: How could Sutter legally claim this land and sell it, in turn, to speculators who, in turn, were again selling the land at outlandish prices?

Moreover, Sutter's grant had been given under Mexican title. That title had been clouded by Mexico's cession of its lands to the United States, the settlers claimed. The question they put: did this not make Sutter's claims invalid and the land public?

The festering quarrel came to a head when the settlers on one side held open public meetings, threatening to defend their lands under squatters' rights,

In this notice, the Settlers' Association gave word to newcomers that the land around Sacramento City was free.

76

and the landed speculators on the other side, formed a Law and Order Association and organized a militia.

The incidents which triggered open battle were three-fold: (1) A group of land speculators took upon themselves the authority to tear down a fence a squatter had built. (2) In the second week of August, County Judge E. J. Willis found a squatter guilty of trespassing and would not suspend execution of his judgment pending an appeal in the courts by the squatters. (3) The squatters, feeling driven to the wall, declared in open meeting they were prepared for the ultimate—warfare—if they could not be heard and their claims judged by higher courts.

The issue which brought on the fighting was a sort of test case which both sides considered crucial to resolution of the difference.

In May 1850, an action was begun against John T. Madden in Recorder's Court, charging Madden with unlawful occupation of a lot on the southeast corner of 2nd and N. The court ruled against Madden. County Judge Willis, newly elected, sustained the judgment on August 8.

Fighting and Peace

As early as the end of 1850 the city was an active, dramatic place with a protective levee and stores with convenient awnings.

Dr. Charles Robinson, later governor of Kansas, was the apparent leader of the settlers in the question of free soil.

The settlers distributed handbills charging "brute force" was being used by the speculators, and insisting the speculators—not the settlers—were inciting riot by "extortion from the timid." The handbill warned that the settlers were determined to "fight with our lives."

It read: "Should such be rendered necessary by the acts of the sheriff or others, the settlers will be governed by martial law."

It also said: "The property and lives of those who take the field against [the settlers] will share the fate of war."

Settlers met at the levee on August 10 under the leadership of Dr. Charles Robinson, who later was to become a member of the California Legislature and, still later, governor of Kansas.

Robinson called for resistance and enlisted an organized company to counter the forces raised by the land speculators. A man named Maloney, a veteran of the Mexican War, commanded the Settlers Company.

Trouble was averted that day when Mayor Hardin Bigelow gave his assurance no writs would be served for arrest. The next day, however, warrants were issued for the arrest of several men who had opposed the sheriff when he endeavored to execute "a writ of restitution of a house held by John T. Madden."

James McClatchy was one of those named in the writ. The other was Richard Moran. McClatchy had arrived in Sacramento the previous June from New York where he had been a correspondent for the *Tribune* edited by Horace Greeley. Moran had arrived some months before the squatter troubles.

Neither Robinson nor McClatchy, both Free Soil advocates, was engaged in property development, nor was either seeking to acquire property for himself.

Together they founded the *Settlers and Miners Tribune*, a new newspaper created to fight monopoly in the land and to carry the fight against land monopoly and the exhorbitant prices speculation triggered. They felt deeply that the frontier should be in the public domain.

In the difficulties which followed, Moran and McClatchy answered the writ, surrendering themselves on August 13 to the authorities. They were placed in the city's prison brig, the *La Grange*. As it was to develop, neither was to be engaged personally in the street fights.

The next day, August 14, Maloney rallied his forces and marched toward the river, apparently intent upon rescuing the prisoners and repossessing the Madden property. The attack on the jail did not develop. It was while the settlers were marching from the Embarcadero to Fourth and J that the fight broke out.

The details are hazy. The *Placer Times* of August 15 reported, to paraphrase a rather involved account, the following story:

Mayor Bigelow had requested that citizens aid to suppress what he feared could be open riot. At 4th and J the mayor ordered the squatters to give up their arms and disperse. Shooting began. The mayor fell from his horse; Maloney was fatally shot through the head. J. W. Woodland, the city assessor, was killed by a stray ball; a Jesse Morgan, in the squatter party, was struck by a ball in the neck, and was killed. Dr. Robinson fell wounded.

The day after the August 14 street battle, Sheriff McKinney, with a posse of twenty men, stormed a settlers' retreat near Brighton, to Sacramento's east, and in the gunfire which followed, McKinney and three settlers died.

This ended the exchange. Peace followed, albeit a shaky peace. In all, eight had died and six had been injured.

With Bigelow wounded, Demas Strong, president of the Common Council, became acting mayor. McClatchy and Moran were released from the prison brig two days after the riot.

Meantime, Robinson was arraigned on a charge of murder, growing out of the riots, but he was never to be brought to trial. Instead, so strong was the sentiment in favor of the settlers—and of Robinson—that his friends put his name up for the State Legislature, and while in prison he was elected.

Sacramento, which had grown too big for Sutter, now had grown too big for speculation.

The year of 1850 was immensely significant to the futures of both California and Sacramento.

On October 15 at two o'clock in the morning, the riverboat *New World* arrived in Sacramento with news that California had been admitted to the Union. It was news that California had awaited for months. Thus Congress moved quickly to bind its newly won territory to the family of states—and thereby discourage any claims on the rich new territory.

Part of the folklore of Sacramento is the report the *New World* brought in newspapers from New York reporting on the admission. It said that men raced on horseback through the streets hawking papers with the declaration: "California is admitted.—Queen Victoria has another baby."

Four years later, Sacramento was to be designated capital of the new state.

But the *New World* was the carrier of something other than good news. It also brought the bad news of cholera to Sacramento.

The first case was reported on October 20, and before the epidemic was to run its course 500 persons were to be stricken—many of them to be buried in a common grave in the new cemetery in the southern environs of the city.

Panic reigned. Many fled. Contemporary accounts suggest some 80 per cent of the population left the city. Deaths were reaching the staggering figure of some 60 a day, and money could not buy nursing, so few were left in the city to attend the stricken.

Among the dead were 17 physicians who did stay, and Mayor Bigelow succumbed to the disease in San Francisco while recuperating from the wounds he received in the Squatter Riot on Sacramento streets. Those who remained rather than fleeing included members of the Masons and I.O.O.F. Lodges—both of which were newly organized—who helped to care for the stricken and assisted their families in a magnificent show of courage and concern.

This would not be the end to Sacramento's baptisms of trial in those founding, cradle years. But it had met test by fire, street warfare and epidemic, and had survived—and had become a legend with a name which, in 1850, already was known on all the civilized continents of the world.

Statehood and Survival

Hardin Bigelow, popular first mayor of Sacramento, never regained health after being wounded in the Squatters Riot.

PART TWO

Growth of a City

*Transportation was the lifeline not only for the miners far away
in the Sierra but for the cities and towns along the rivers and
the way stations inland. The river was the prime artery for years
before the wagon routes and then the railroad. Sacramento
was the major California point for all three. Above is a
painting of the Sacramento station by William Hahn.*

Introduction

Sutter had been right.
    The city's future, he had said,
    lay in the land,
    not in the Mother Lode
    —its treasure soon would peter out
    and only tailings would remain.
    But land;
    now that is different, Sutter said.
    Land would yield a fortune far more precious
    and of much firmer stuff
    than all the gold mined by the Argonaut
    in the Sierra diggings.
    And he was right.

But a city is built of more than land or timber hewn
    or iron nails driven.
    It is built, as well, of pins and string
    and fine-spun thread
    —of wire for fence,
    —salt for pork,
    —handle for hoe
    —and out of bolts of gingham dear to her
    who left her world behind
    and with her man, settled here.

Yes, a city is built by merchant
    as well as by carpenter.
    He it is who brings the pins
    and string and thread.
    He seeks the coin of commerce,
    and in the seeking, builds.
    He was here to greet the Argonaut
    and here offered his wares
    spread out on flatboats on the river,
    and then stayed to prosper.

*Artist William Hahn made visual and audible
the frantic activity of the Sacramento railroad station
in its heyday of the 1870s.*

83

In 1859, Hubbard's Garden opened a mile-and-a-half from town. On Sundays, it offered "a strong police force to preserve order." The "garden" form of entertainment came to California in the 1850s from London, and several were in operation by 1857.

This view of Sacramento's waterfront is reputed to have been painted between 1855 and 1860 by George Tirrell. The sidewheeler just to the right of center is the Antelope, and the many ships testify to the intense activity in the young city.

Tirrell later became famous for painting the longest panorama ever done. It was 25,300 square feet of California scenes and took an entire evening to unroll at its first showing in San Francisco in 1860.

Dr. Thomas M. Logan painted a prize-winning exhibit from Smith's Gardens in 1855. It was such an impressive rendering that it was lithographed several times to promote the agriculture of the region. Smith's Gardens produced outstanding products from the rich soil near the American River.

City of the Plain

By the year 1857, when George H. Baker published his beautiful
City of the Plain, *the frontier village of Sacramento City had forgotten the
infancy it was permitted for such a short time. Not even a decade had passed and
the pioneer hamlet of the City Hotel and the Eagle Theater had grown to
such an extent and developed so in sophisticated architecture that it presented the
picture shown here. Still, no bridge spanned the Sacramento at this time,
and all crossings were by way of ferry boats.*

*Baker's meticulous effort is clearly evident
in these details from the larger work. Sacramento was
even then obviously a city planning to stay.*

87

Life in the Community

SACRAMENTO HAD EVERYTHING going for it in the early decades of its settlement, first as outpost, then as gateway to the rich Sierra diggings, and finally as merchandising, agricultural, and theater center for a valley rich in promise and in trade.

In 1850, the official United States Census for the City and County of Sacramento totaled 9,087 persons; in 1852, the state census revealed a population of 12,418.

This is a head count of only those who gave the city or the county as their place of residence. It does not include the thousands who stopped over in the city—some briefly, some for long periods of time—on their way to the gold fields. Or those who stopped just long enough to turn around and leave, disillusioned.

As an indication of the kind of business the city was doing in the early 1850s, there is the record that in the year 1852–53, April to April, 410 vessels arrived at the Embarcadero and delivered, for Sacramento use, some 165,000 tons of freight. As a further indication of its increasing ability to provide for itself—in terms of flour, wheat, barley; of salmon, lumber, lime; and in the many other provisions that were important to the new city—Sacramento imported less than 98,550 tons of goods in the year 1854–55, April to April, despite the fact its population, of course, was increasing.

So promising was the agricultural outlook, in fact, it moved *Sacramento Illustrated* to predict, correctly, that one day soon Sacramento would be exporting, not importing, wares. In a rather generous estimate, it spoke of Sacramento and California: "A country that has raised eighty-three bushels of wheat to the acre, and beets seven feet in length, and other productions of like nature, must yet astonish the world, not only with its mineral but agricultural wealth."

In this same period, 1854–55, the Sierra diggings still were yielding in abundance. Gold dust deposits were averaging around $3,000,000 and the city was doing about $6,000,000 in trade each month.

Even in that early hour of the city's history there were those who were thinking beyond, into tomorrow, and envisioning the bridging of the Sierra

This sketch by Emil Lehman shows the temporary nature
of those who lived under canvas and stars. The lady of the house
stands primly under a valley oak.   89

with rail. In a rather offhand gesture, one publication speculated: "If necessary, a five-mile tunnel can be cut through the Sierra Nevada. Already twice that amount has been tunneled in the mountains by the enterprising miners of Mameluke Hill. All that is needed is for Congress to give the same encouragement that has been extended by nature to the miner and it will be done. . . ."

Boom and Speculation

In October, 1849, Sacramento's population had increased from the original handful at the fort to some 2,000, and was a "city" of some 45 wooden buildings and 300 cloth houses, including campsites under trees along the river and inland. Two months later, the population had almost doubled to 3,500.

This was the city scene in part, '49 vintage.

Among the principal buildings then in town were the zinc warehouse, near the outlet of Sutter's Lake; Montgomery and Warbous' Zinc Store, and the Empire Saloon, on J Street, between Front and 2nd; the City Hotel on the levee; Merritt's brick building on the corner of J and 2nd streets; the Sutter House on Front Street between K and L; the brick block on Front Street between N and O; the Irving House on J Street between 3rd and 4th; Haycock's store, corner of J and 3rd streets; and Drs. Morse and Stillman's Hospital, corner of K and 3rd streets.

The Common Council moved at this time, moreover, to establish fees for license. Tax on wholesale and retail trade was set at $50 a month; on hotels and eating houses, $25; on bars and coffee stands, $50; on faro and gaming tables, $30; on billiard tables, $20; on concerts or public entertainments, $5. And, yes, on bowling alleys, $10.

The council also decided councilmen should be paid, and so accordingly it voted each member $100 a month salary. This did not set well; there was a citizen movement, in rebellion, and a new charter was urged upon the State Legislature; the reform, sans the generous $100 salary, was approved.

To gain an appreciation of how swiftly the city had taken form, how diversified was its business, there were these firms already established in 1850: Hensley & Reading; Brannan & Sherwood; Orland McKnight; Powers & Perkins; Henley & Birdsall; Earl McIntosh & Co.; Moran & Clark; Samuel Gregg; S. C. Bruce; Montgomery & Co.; Barton Lee; S. Brannan & Co.; Burnett Ferguson & Co.; Beyer Simmons; Mellus, Howard & Co.; Haywood, Peachy & Co.; H. E. Robinson; Hanner, Jennings & Co.; Paul, White & Co. to name but a few.

It was a time, too, of speculation, of inflation. Property values skyrock-

George H. Baker captured the changes in Sacramento between 1849 (right) and 1855 (next page). The trees were gone and there were multistoried buildings by 1855.

eted, but the higher the price the more spirited the competition. There was this view:

"In this inflated condition of affairs, the most perfect security was manifest, and the most wild and moonshine speculations were indulged in, and all seemed to forget that the day of reckoning must surely come—when monthly, ten and fifteen per cent interest, must be paid, and property be sold to the highest bidder."

The first indication there was a ceiling beyond which even the gold city economy could not be pushed came with the failure in 1850 of one of the most respected banking houses, Barton Lee, which represented a capital of nearly $1,500,000. Then followed failures of the banking house of Hensley, McKnight & Hastings, followed by the House of Warbass & Co. A wave of doubt began to curb ventures in the new city, and only gold, for a time, was not suspect. The doubt was shortlived, however. Soon confidence was restored. Business boomed as the harvest in the Sierra boomed. Sacramento, the city, collected going and coming. As portal to the rich northern fields, it was provision post for miners bound for the Sierra; as river port, it was departure post for those who hit it big and for those who hit it middlin', as they used to say, and for those who, skunked and disappointed, were anxious to return home.

More Solid Foundations

But a careful tracing of Sacramento's business and commercial growth in the building years is essential to the more complete record. Sometimes those records are not as precise as one would wish. Example: Three structures are said to have occupied the northeast corner of Front and J by the end of 1851, each in its turn more ambitious. The illustrator George V. Cooper showed a three-story building containing offices and a supply store occupied by an S. Taylor. There is reason to believe the building never was completed, as the Cooper view indicated, for it was blown down by a strong wind when in skeletal form in the fall of 1849, according to newspaper sources. The speculation is that Cooper roughly sketched the print here, then finished it in the East unaware that the corner building in his city scene never had been finished. Of such fragile threads is the fabric of history sometimes stitched. Actually, the sequence was thus: In December, 1849, an attorney, Samuel C. Bruce, put up a two-story building called the Tehama Block on the corner. The impressive flood-period lithograph of Casselear and Bainbridge shows the building was operated by G. S. Stevens when the flood struck in January, 1850. In early 1851, the building had become the depot for distribution of the *True Delta*, a New Orleans news-

The Tehama Block on the northeast corner of Front and J contained offices for attorneys and was the distribution point for a New Orleans newspaper, the *True Delta*.

paper, with legal offices on the second floor. But by mid-1851 the building was razed to make way for the long-lasting—and second—Tehama Block which was to become familiar as the site of such early city operations as Dankel's; Page, and Bacon; Adams & Company, and G. Frank Smith. The change is synonymous with change throughout the burgeoning city in that time of building.

Across the street, on the southeast corner of Front and J, Sam Brannan's store remained but it became the Mansion House. The Embarcadero still was the focal point in the city life, and the city was growing much as an inverted "T" with Front and J the convergence. Buildings shoulder to shoulder faced the river along Front from Hensley and Reading's pioneer store at I, southward past L, where they then thinned out perhaps to as far as O. J exploded on both sides to about 3rd in the first year of the city, then underwent a slower, more orderly growth which found it lined with buildings as far as 7th or 8th by 1854. K lagged J in development, holding short of 2nd for the first year or so, but 2nd became a bustling business street by mid-1850 and soon outstripped Front in growth and promise. But for all development, the story was the same. The miners were coming in force and the demand they created for goods could not be met swiftly enough; and with the demand came a spawned growth in the new city, fantastic in its promise of fortune.

And it all began on the riverbank. Here, in a short-term operation, merchants set up makeshift displays for their wares and erected crude warehouses for storage. All of this gave off the atmosphere of an open bazaar with miners sometimes buying provisions from boxes never opened and fighting for the chance to buy.

One such mercantile outlet was the *Lady Adams*, a brig which was to be the namesake for the Lady Adams Mercantile Co. at 115 K. It still stands, albeit but a shell of its original grandeur—the oldest building remaining in the city outside of Sutter's Fort and the only building still standing to survive the 1852 fire which leveled seven-eighths of the city.

Its story is symbolic of the merchandising romance which attended the origins. It goes back to a time when merchants were bidding $3,000 to $5,000 for 25-foot frontages and were paying up to $500 per thousand board feet for lumber.

It was August 1849 when a brig bearing the courtly name *Lady Adams* sailed into San Francisco Bay, then up the Sacramento inbound from a Peruvian seaport. Its original embarkation port: Unknown. But on board was a company of German immigrants, among them the ship's owners. Arriving in Sacramento, they snubbed the *Lady Adams* to moorings at the foot of K where its owners converted it into a floating mercantile store stocked with wares they had brought in the passage around the Horn. The original members of that firm were Christian (Carl) Ihmels, Nicholas T. Stockfleth, and Julius Politz. In the next two years, Francis (Frederick) Bartels joined the firm, by then known throughout the gold country.

In 1852 the partners negotiated to buy a lot a stone's throw from the brig to build a permanent store. The address was 13 and 15 K by the early numbering system. It rose, this newest of Sacramento's business houses, as a two-story brick construction, simple in lines and 45 by 75 feet. It cost $40,000. And part of the legend that has survived the *Lady Adams* is that it is literally true the Lady Adams store was shipped around the Horn, for the brick used in its construction was brick which had been stored in the hold of the *Lady Adams* brig for ballast. A dismantled boom taken from the *Lady Adams* was laid in the gutter in front of the building to form a buffer against which the wheels of delivery wagons could rest. When the smoke of the 1852 fire cleared, the Lady Adams Building, with few others, still stood. In fact, the 1856 *City Directory* said of it: "It is looked upon as a landmark of the city's primitive architecture."

At about the time of the Lady Adams construction, downtown Sacramento was beginning to take on a more permanent look. The unpainted structures of 1849 hardly sufficed. The vagabond miner was inclined to take his business to the store which made some attempt at civilized merchandising and cosmetics, even if the paint was only whitewash. And there are accounts which tell us the gambling halls and saloons, almost predictably, were the first to offer the touch of luxury. The El Dorado Saloon, for example, is said to have offered a decor luxurious enough to calm the monte player who had lost his diggings and had to set out again to work up another stake.

Curiously, even as early as March 1851 the *Sacramento Transcript* was lamenting that the "new" city was not made of the grander stuff of "Old Sacramento." It complained that miners in the beginning did all their business in "dust," but

of S.	Mulattoes, male,	80
	do female,	18
the	do over 21 years of age	84
in a	Indians, male,	62
ʼablo	do female,	18
feet	do over 21 years of age.	38
Las	Foreign residents, male,	971
ʼ the	do do female,	281
ough	do do over 21 years,	1015
ence	Chinese,	804
icra-	do male,	794
rs in	do female,	10

<table>
<tr><td colspan="2">Productions and Capital.</td></tr>
<tr><td>No Horses,</td><td>3729</td></tr>
<tr><td>" Mules,</td><td>1190</td></tr>
<tr><td>" Cows,</td><td>3945</td></tr>
<tr><td>" Beef Cattle,</td><td>3718</td></tr>
<tr><td>" Work Oxen,</td><td>2057</td></tr>
<tr><td>" Sheep,</td><td>3077</td></tr>
<tr><td>" Hogs,</td><td>4617</td></tr>
<tr><td>" Poultry,</td><td>16,228</td></tr>
<tr><td>Bushels Barley,</td><td>157,071</td></tr>
<tr><td>" Oats,</td><td>10,760</td></tr>
<tr><td>" Corn,</td><td>1247</td></tr>
<tr><td>" Wheat,</td><td>14,290</td></tr>
<tr><td>" Potatoes,</td><td>28,204</td></tr>
<tr><td>Tons Hay,</td><td>10,042</td></tr>
<tr><td>Total value of live stock,</td><td>1,335,698</td></tr>
<tr><td>do do agricultural prodts,</td><td>737,643</td></tr>
</table>

Horticulture.	
Beets,	612,295 lbs.
Onions,	713,750 "
Cabbage,	1,817,750 "
Tomatoes,	1,039,800 "
Carrots,	107,500 "
Parsnips,	60,650 "
Pumpkins,	460,100 "
Turnips,	356,600 "
Melons,	358 acres.
Total value,	$339,682 00
Am't generally invested,	$5,358,394
" in quartz mining,	124,165
" in Placer mining,	89,808
" other mining operations,	169,850
" Stock,	1,335,698
" Farming,	737,643
" Gardening,	339,682
Total,	$8,155,241

SAN JOAQUIN COUNTY.

Population,	5029
White male inhabitants,	3582

A portion of a census taken by the state in 1852 shows amazing growth in three years.

Dollars Instead of Ounces

93

SACRAMENTO TRANSCRIPT

VOLUME I.   SACRAMENTO CITY, CALIFORNIA, MAY 21, 1850.   NUMBER 22.

coin in 1851 was greasing the wheels of commerce. In a remarkable appraisal published March 8 of that year the *Transcript* said:

How things have changed in one year. One does not see the old greasy buckskin now, filled to the brim with the glittering dust. Those were the good old times, when the miners paid for everything in dust—when the red-shirted gentry were the nabobs of the land—when the dirty shirt and coatless party, were worth their thousands. It may seem strange, yet it is not the less true, that thousands of persons in this state last fall a year did not own a coat, and yet they may have had several thousand dollars in the pocket ... What a happy and glorious state of morals were universally prevalent. Then, every one regarded his neighbor as honest until adverse proof was aduced. Stores were in canvass houses with no protection watever [sic]. Safes, lockes and all othose fixings used to guard against thieves, were unknown.

These days have passed and with the change has come idle vagrancy, and coin as a circulating medium. Instead of that free and carefree spirit of spending money, men now regard dollars as much as they once esteemed ounces. They grip a dollar with more tenacity than they formerly did their pounds of dust. Instead of the old time apparel, nothing will do now but clothes of the fanciest hue and finest fabric, and "tiles" of the latest and most fashionable style. We doubt indeed whether there is a more rigid adherence to fashion anywhere, than is now visible in the resident population of Sacramento ... We sigh for a return of those days when the old buckskin purse used to be fished up from the hidden recesses of a pocket where its companions were a jackknife, nails, tobacco, &c, &c.

The Woman's View

The Gold Rush which spurred the growth of a city by the Embarcadero and spawned an industry throughout the mountains largely was, by nature of the times, a masculine event. However, women were not totally absent. There were those of doubtful vocations, of course; they will be found in any boom town. There were others, not numerous, but conspicuous; and their influence in bringing civilization to the region perhaps never can be assessed properly.

The woman who accompanied her man to the gold country in the 1850s had to have stamina and inner strength—and be more self-sufficient than her counterpart of this century could possibly imagine.

Her ambitions were for the little things: a bolt of gingham for a new dress, the comfort of another woman nearby to share the intimate secrets a woman will share only with another woman, a smattering of medicines for the emergencies which inevitably beset a family.

What was life for a woman in the sparsely settled region around Sacramento and in the nearby gold country? Perhaps the best revelation is to be found in the so-called Shirley letters written by Louisa A. Clappe, wife of a young physician who went to the mines in Plumas County in 1851. She wrote:

"How would you like to winter in such an abode? In a place where there are no newspapers, no churches, lectures, concerts or theaters; no fresh books, no shopping, no picnics, no tableaux, no charades, no latest fashions, no daily mail (we have an express once a month), no promenades, no rides nor drives; no vegetables, but potatoes and onions, no milk, no eggs, no nothing."

She described her day as getting up at dawn and going to bed almost at sundown. Candles were too precious to be burned without good reason. Her day, she said, was made up of cleaning her home, a 20-foot square cabin divided into two rooms by a flowered curtain. When she had completed her work, there was little else to do.

Her home probably was typical of the gold country at that time: makeshift, temporary. Her letters described it thus. "The room into which we have just entered is about 20 feet square. It is lined over the top with cotton cloth, the breadths of which being sewed together only in spots stretch gracefully apart in many places, giving one a bird's eye view of the shingles above. The sides are hung with gaudy chintz. A curtain of the above described chintz divides off a portion of the room, behind which stands a bedstead that in ponderosity leaves the Empire [a hotel] couches far behind."

Moreover, a woman who set up housekeeping in that day had to be resourceful, for her problems were many. The diary of one woman, a Mrs. Susan Kuykendall, indicates some of the collected wisdom of the pioneer woman. Some of her homemaking hints, probably common to her time, follow:

Corn—Soaking corn in salt petre is said to be a great remedy to prevent the birds from taking it.

Flies—To remove flies from rooms take one-fourth teaspoonful of black pepper, one of brown sugar, one tablespoon of cream, mix them well together and place them on a plate in a room where the flies are and they will soon disappear.

Sacramento in the fifties appears to have had very busy streets and hectic traffic.

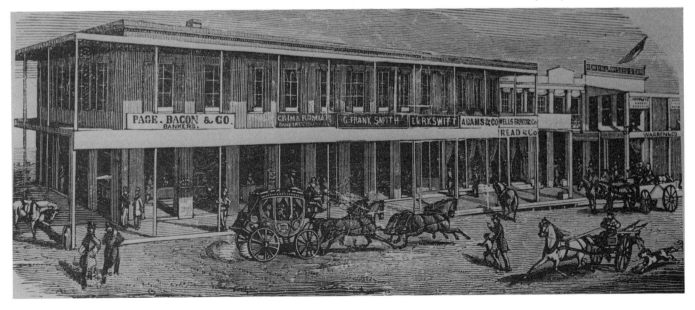

Cleaning knives and forks—Charcoal ground to powder is one of the best things ever discovered to clean knives; this is a late and valuable discovery.

Candles—Take one pound of alum and one pound of salt petre, dissolve them together in a pint of water; melt 12 pounds of lard, then add both together, simmer them till the water is evaporated, then mold the candles.

Fattening poultry—An excellent way is to boil potatoes and mash them fine, then add meat just before the food is given to them; it is asserted that turkeys and geese and other fowls will thus fatten in one-half the time usually required when they are fed on grain alone.

Bugs—To get rid of bedbugs and other bugs, gather a handful of smart weed, boil in one pint of water and when cold rub with the liquid where they frequent and they will soon disappear.

*Hostelries:
Fort to Hotels*

Within two years the city had outgrown its "T" configuration. Substantial building was to be found lining I, J, K, and L with other stores and homes scattered east and south.

By 1852 Sutter's Fort, citadel and rendezvous point for so many in the pre-gold settlement, now was all but abandoned. An 1852 description went: "Decay sat queen in the once proud castle. The massive gates were broken and gone. The roofs were breaking and falling through. . . . There were none to

96

Emil Lehman was a Sacramento visitor in 1852. The artist, thought to have been Swedish, left little knowledge of himself but a rich source of Sacramento life in his drawings. Sometime after he did the scene above, he refined the left portion in the more detailed drawing below.

Lehman looked south and west from the corner of 3rd and J, and in the drawing above the river is visible at the foot of J. The drawing below looks south on 3rd, in a more finished version drawn later from the original sketch.

The two sketches above were done on J between 3rd and 4th just months before the devastation of the fire. The sketch at right is coded for color, and the dome Lehman drew in is a mystery.

raise the 'flag of the free' over the fast-coming ruin, where so long it waved in triumph.''

The fort had been reduced to history, a watering hole of brief life, in three short years. The city, not the fort, was now the future.

Furthermore, the early businesses which probably thrived the best were those which catered to the transient population: hotels, provision houses, express companies, financial institutions.

The City Hotel and the Hotel de France were pioneers in this venture. Significantly, they fronted on the river whence came their trade. The de France was the first to rise, built by John Fowler and Sam Brannan in 1849. It opened next to the Eagle Theater with a huge champagne party; shortly, the City Hotel rose nearby, a touchstone of civilization with a rather swaggering manner when one considered the wilderness surroundings.

The next permanent hotel to go up was of special significance, for it was the city's first brick construction. Raised in 1850, it was built by George Zins of brick he manufactuered himself near Sutterville. It was known first as the Anchor House, then as the Green Tree, finally as the Pioneer. Its location was Front and M. Other construction followed—too swiftly to chronicle simply.

The Elephant House was on Front between J and K, prominent in early city drawings and called the "palace" hotel of its day, even though it offered only tiers of bunks for sleeping. The Sutter Hotel, which rose on Front between K and L, had more substantial offerings. It rose three stories and boasted full living accommodation.

The business of lodging could not be contained on Front for long. In 1850, along with many small establishments, two large hotels stood on J between 3rd and 4th, the Crescent City and the Missouri, both doomed to destruction in the

fire of 1852. It was not much later that the lodging business extended even farther east on J with the Abbey Hotel, between 6th and 7th, and the Union rising between 7th and 8th.

Second Street was salted with hotels shortly, too. The Verandah, later replaced by another Union Hotel, was between J and K next to one of the city's most venerable establishments, the Orleans. The Orleans brought a Creole touch to the city, having been shipped from New Orleans around the Horn,

The crude interior of an unidentified store interested the artist. Goods are displayed everywhere, and on the wall is what may be a portrait of George Washington.

pre-cut and ready for assembly. When this landmark burned in the 1852 fire, a new brick structure was begun almost before the embers cooled; and bearing the same name it was to be the most prominent hostelry of its period. Advertisements boasted a reading room, billiard room, and saloon as well as "second and third stories . . . set apart for parlor, family rooms and chambers." Eventually it was to serve as headquarters for the California Stage Company as well.

Other memorable structures of that time, familiar to the early history, include scores more. To name a few: the Golden Eagle on K near 7th; the Clarendon between K and L on 2nd; the Dawson House, later known as the St. George, at 4th and J; and the What Cheer House, a public meeting place of renown which started out with the somewhat unromantic name of Sackett's Hotel, and became the Grand Hotel after the Civil War.

To Serve A City

But a city is more than a place for transients to find overnight lodgings or a quick bite. The growth beyond to 8th and south to O and P involved more than hotels and restaurants. There were provision merchants, first represented by George McDougal's supply ship moored at the Embarcadero and then by Hensley and Reading with their first building at Front and I.

Sam Brannan outfitted miners from the southeast corner of Front and J; and first a Mr. Taylor, then a Mr. Stevens did the same thing on the opposite corner. J. B. Starr was busy auctioning goods right off the boats or selling them wholesale at his place at Front and K. Reed, Grimm and Co. were competing with him at Front and the Miners' Variety Store, owned by L. Prince, offered everything from wheelbarrows to Colt revolvers on J below 3rd in the early days; in the next block was Sheldon, Kibbe and Almy, offering similar goods.

Within a couple of years, general provisions also could be purchased from Hoope & L'Amoureux at J and 6th, Haskell and Co. on K above 3rd, and Hermance and Burton on J near 4th. Three Stanford Brothers opened their store on K and 3rd about this time and soon another brother would join them, and then a fifth, Leland, and much would be heard about him in the years to come.

Supply centers for the miners, banks, and assay offices were numerous among the early businesses, as were express companies, attorney firms, pharmacies, and other firms catering to the miners. B. F. Hastings and D. O. Mills opened pioneer financial houses which became strong economic forces in later years. Hastings was on 2nd Street and Mills on J. And from his first bank, built in Sacramento, Mills was to build a financial institution which was to command a national reputation in banking. A. M. Winn was a general land agent and political leader of the city who, in 1850, headquartered on M between 2nd and 3rd. J. Neely Johnson, later governor of California, had law offices on 3rd near J in those early years, while transportation offices could be found on J between 3rd and 4th in the form of Hawley and Company; and James Birch ran a successful freight line into the Sierra from the Sutter Hotel on Front before starting the California Stage Company later.

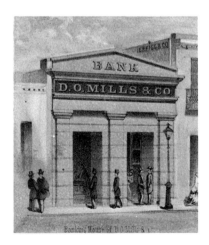

By 1852, the ramshackle and makeshift early construction had vanished, and in its place rose a variety of competing merchandising and service houses. Miners Drug, operated by R. H. McDonald, stood between 5th and 6th on J,

Union Pacific Railroad photographer
A. J. Russell took this view of K at Front
in 1870. Though the glass plate he used
is damaged, the picture is very clear. In
the background is the spire of St. Rose
of Lima and just behind the balcony at
left is the Lady Adams Building, the
oldest in the city still standing.

and Polhemus Drug was at 190 J. They were the city's leading dispensers of
medicines, but there were others. Clothing stores, by 1852, were plentiful. By
then, even vanity houses, featuring exotic feminine items, were present: Victor
Passenaurd's City of Paris, and others. Heavy industry was present, as well, in
the form of the Eureka Iron and Brass Foundry on Front between O and P, Van
Winkle and Duncan, agents for imported iron, and the brass foundry of Lambard and Goss at 2nd and I.

That new wonder, the tin-type picture, was a Sacramento delight also.
Charles King offered this new service from a studio at 130 K and Beal's Da-
guerrean Gallery was operating at 87 J. Earlier, George H. Johnson had brought
his photo machine to the city, before moving on to San Francisco.

A more basic type of business, one which had attracted even the Indians
before Sutter, took its place in the economic structure of the new city. It may
be difficult to imagine it now, but there was a time when the waters of the
Sacramento and the American rivers were as clear as crystal, and burdened with
fish. Small wonder the Indian colonies before the advent of Western man fat-
tened off the rich harvest; small wonder those who came here to found a new
empire would turn to the rivers with nets. By 1851 they were fishing the Sacramento 50 miles above and below the confluence with the American, and the
American toward its watersheds. The *Placer Times and Transcript* said in 1851
of the Salmon catch: "... in the spring and summer [fishing] gives profitable

This daguerreotype by George H. Johnson was taken at 4th and J in 1852 or earlier. At left is what appears to be a used wagon lot, with prices affixed to each wagon on sale. The Oriental Hotel is in the background.

occupation to several hundred persons. Hundreds of this choice species of the finny tribe are caught daily in front of the city, weighting from 10 to 80 pounds each, besides an immense quantity of sturgeon, perch, and other fish."

John Sutter had recognized this natural resource. The Swedish scholar known as the King's Orphan took note of it in 1843 when he wrote, ". . . he [Sutter] has realized considerable income from the salmon fisheries of the rivers, the fish being unequalled in flavor and found in the greatest abundance."

George Cooper was the first to pack fish for marketing in 1851. The economic importance of fisheries—with increasing exports to the East—was detailed in the *Sacramento Directory* of 1858. It reported 1½ million pounds of fish had been caught the year before and sold at a price of 3¢ a pound. The Sacramento fisheries were described as the greatest in their time on the Pacific Coast.

It was not Sacramento's destiny, then as now, to become an industrial city but that is not to say it was without industry.

Molds and machinery arrived in April of 1850 from Chicago for the California Steam Engine Works of Stow and Carpenter at Front and Sycamore, near the mouth of the American River. Work was plentiful as the demands of the mines grew. Taylor and Woods put the Eureka Iron and Brass Foundry into operation in September of 1851 on Front between O and P. The following year, James Bowstead entered the management, and it became a major factory, in 1855 building the machinery for some 28 large mills and many smaller ones to produce such divergent products as quartz, lumber, malt, cement, and many others. In 1857, Bowstead established the Union Foundry on Front between N and O, but the Eureka continued under Wilson and Company.

Sacramento Iron Works on I between Front and 2nd began operation in 1852 and brought to its proprietors, Lambard and Goss, much praise. It was a leading employer by 1860, and before another decade passed, its payroll included a hundred men. The *City Directory* of 1868 placed it "in the front rank of that class of establishment on the coast," and reported its engines and pestles were stamping quartz throughout much of California and Nevada.

M. R. Rose opened the Capital Iron and Brass Works on K between 9th and 10th in 1862, and in 1867, William Gutenberger established the Sacramento Foundry at Front and N.

John A. Sutter correctly saw the need for flour milling to supply the growing population of the pre-gold settlement, and for lumber milling. In fact, it was Sutter's ambition to erect a lumber mill in Coloma in 1848 which led to the discovery of gold there and to the Gold Rush itself. Sutter never finished his flour mill on the American River at Brighton, but the lumber already used was purchased by Sam Brannan and used to build the Hotel de France on Front Street. In 1850, Colonel Wilson built the Eureka Flour Mills in Slater's Addition, between I and the American River, where it operated until fire destroyed it in 1856.

R. D. Carey began the Levee Mills in 1853 near the point where the Sacramento and Yolo Bridge later was built. Garfield and Company bought the works in 1856 and renamed it the Pioneer Mills. It was destined to become one of the largest operations in the state. By 1870, the Pioneer was producing 500 barrels per day. The Lambard Mills on I were operated in conjunction with the Sacramento Iron Works for a time.

The Phoenix Flouring Mill opened by a stock company in 1855 at 13th and J. Eventually, W. P. McCreary became sole proprietor and was succeeded by his sons, who sold to Reel and Barber in 1868. The McCrearys, operating under the title of Charles McCreary and Company, then began the Sacramento Flouring Mills on Front between L and M in 1869. The Star Mills went into operation at 7th and J in 1866, but Neubourg and Lages, who specialized in products for brewers, met with such success they moved to 5th between J and

The Stanford Brothers' wholesale provision house operated at Front and L without Leland for awhile when he conducted business in several gold communities.

The Union and Orleans Hotels in 1857 were the most prominent of the day; each was owned by a mayor of the city.

K in 1873. The Sacramento Valley was becoming noted as a wheat bonanza, and the Sacramento mills not only supplied the growing local needs, but also shipped their products all over the world.

Seven separate carriage shops, all capable of both construction and service, boasted products as fine as any in the United States, while 13 shoe and boot shops made Sacramento the largest footwear manufactury west of the Mississippi in the late 1860s. Eleven tailor shops were located in the city, and three cigar manufacturers were busy filling orders by the time the new capitol was complete with cupola.

The miners who made the long and dusty trip down from the hills, along with the travelers who were ending lengthy journeys, created an inordinate demand for beer in early Sacramento. Peter Kadell, a German '49er, sought to supply them from his Sacramento Brewery as early as 1850. Other early brewers were Zins and Weiser, Louis Keseberg, and Philip Yager, the latter establishing his plant in Brannan's old adobe near the ruins of the fort. Of these early breweries, only the Sacramento, purchased in 1854 by Philip Scheld, and the Columbus, started in 1853 by E. and C. Gruhler at 15th and K, enjoyed lasting success. As the city entered the 1870s, these two had been joined by the Pacific Brewery at 9th and P, the City Brewery at 12th and H, the St. Louis at 6th and G, the Capital at 12th and I, and the Sutterville down the river.

There are more examples of industry—too many to provide anything like a complete list—but others include: A steam planing mill at Front and Q opened by Thomas Latta in 1852; a coffee and spice mill operated by Dingley, Heisch and Krenzberger on I below 2nd; and 10 millinery shops along with 15 dressmaking operations to serve the growing female population.

The industry which was to dominate the city, of course, was the railroad, with its accompanying shops and foundries, wheelworks and construction activities. There were maintenance and repair facilities for the Sacramento Valley Rail Road as early as 1855, but the major impact came in the 1860s with the beginning of the Central Pacific. As track was laid eastward, the shop facilities lengthened along the northern edge of China Slough. Even before the tracks joined with those of the Union Pacific, the C.P.R.R. was among the city's leading employers. The shops produced wheels, cars, machine parts, and eventually locomotives in the growing complex of buildings. And within a few years after the completion of the Central Pacific, the corporation took its place as the leading employer in the city.

Sacramento was busy elsewhere, too, making bricks and brooms and barrels and scores of other products for local shops as well as for export. Sacramento had begun as a supply depot and a way station, it is true, but as the years passed the city entered the industrial age on its own terms.

All the while, almost unnoticed in the hubub of the business growth, a residential Sacramento was growing. Modest in its early years, it was to know some mansions before too long. But in the beginning, even some of those who would be giants later on found home and hearth and happiness in much simpler houses.

Mary Crocker, the wife of Charles Crocker, wrote on March 25, 1853, shortly after arriving in Sacramento with her husband:

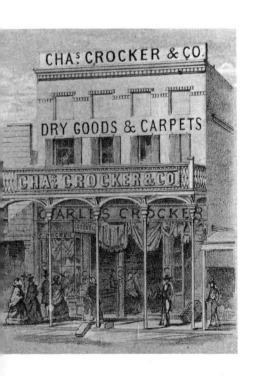

Thursday Charles bought lumber, Friday the men commenced us a house [an addition to Edwin's in the form of a shed or lean-to]. Saturday afternoon I left the hotel where we had boarded at $25 per week and took quiet possession of our own home. We have a nice snug little room; it is lined all over with factory cloth. Our bed is covered with white. I have one window with a white curtain. We have a pretty carpet, one large rocking chair in which I now sit, another chair in front I use for a table (my letter rests on my knee), a large looking glass, a wash stand with white furniture, two trunks and sundry small articles not mentioned.

She did not find it uncomfortable, or the new life without interest. She wrote:

"You can form some idea of my situation from this, but you can't tell how really comfortable and pleasant it is without coming in and seeing. The new part was divided into two bedrooms by a cloth partition, one ours, the other Edwin's. This is California style—all cloth partitions and cloth plastering."

Mrs. Crocker would one day describe much finer accommodations, but she, like all the early arrivals, shared the dramatic experience of growing with a city.

It was not long before the Frontier Town was gone, short-lived and of brief history. The Embarcadero still fed the city, but it no longer dominated it. Shops expanded rapidly eastward and southward in such numbers that it would be exhausting, and to no point, to list all the merchants, even all of the best known, or all of the services offered, even the most elementary. That inverted "T," with its convergence at Front and J soon was lost in the patchwork of a well planned, well developed city extending southward to R, where a railroad soon would swing out to the foothills. Shortly the city took on the substantial look of permanency, but was soon to face a new crisis: Fire.

Some said the glow of the fire on November 2, 1852, could be seen in San Francisco the night Sacramento burned. The tragedy was widely known, and this scene appeared in the *New York Illustrated News*.

Fire and Water

The threat of fire had been very much in Sacramento's thoughts in the building years. There still was a lingering memory of the 1850 fire. By 1852, the city had exploded in population to some 12,000. The settlement was advancing, for the most part, well beyond the canvas and clapboard era of its beginnings, and was starting to take on the look of permanency. But as elsewhere in the north country in the settlement years—San Francisco was leveled twice in its first decades—Sacramento was to be put to the torch. On the night of November 4, seven-eighths of the city was to be burned in one night's holocaust carried on a strong north wind. Damages were to be estimated at bordering six million dollars. The morning brought a scene of wretched destruction—a city left virtually houseless and with fortunes wiped out between dusk and dawn.

The *Daily Union* account read, in part:

"That terrible destroyer, which has heretofore laid in ashes every important town in this State, has at last visited our fair 'City of the Plains' and in a few brief hours swept almost every vestige of it from existence."

The fire broke out at 10 minutes past 11 o'clock on a Tuesday night in a millinery shop operated by a Madame Lanas on the north side of J near 4th. A north wind, at near-gale strength, quickly carried the fire through the city; contemporary accounts reported burning planks were whisked about like sticks, with debris lighting the sky. Fire fastened onto the vulnerable and frail wood structures so recently put up, enveloping them.

In minutes Madame Lanas' shop and the Southern House, a large frame hotel nearby, were reduced to ash. The building of Hart, Alpin and Company, a paint shop, and an establishment operated by a Mr. Passenaurd, perfumer, perished. Quickly the Crescent City Hotel was in flames.

Gone in the morning also were such new enterprises as the Missouri Hotel;

Nevitt and Company, a hardware enterprise; the Phoenix Hotel; the Methodist Church; the Roman Catholic Church; the Baptist Church; Brown, Henry & Company, a dry goods firm; Mitchell & Company, shoe dealers; W. R. Hopkins Company, wholesale dealers in dry goods; the city's post office; the Overton Block; and on through the directory.

Surviving because of their construction were Bushness & Company, J. Madison, Watson & Biscol, the Lady Adams Building, and the Stanford Brothers Store. Only the Lady Adams Building, of all those on the 1852 scene, still stands in the city's cradleground.

The reconstruction following the flaming destruction was rapid and complete. Those pioneers were not given to long periods of mourning. Just two years later, in 1854, with the downtown so newly rebuilt, fire struck again, devastatingly. The better portion of twelve blocks was leveled to ash when flames swept down I and J streets as well as the north side of K from just above 3rd, eastward to 17th. It was 1852 repeated.

There is an episode of the 1854 fire which deserves retelling.

Governor Bigler was seeking to recruit volunteers to help save the courthouse. Several demurred. They had their own buildings to look after, they protested. A full-length portrait of George Washington was housed in the courthouse. Bigler snapped: "See! There is the portrait of the father of your country. Will you permit it to be destroyed?" There was a rush to salvage the courthouse, so it is said, but only the picture and a few other artifacts were saved; the building perished.

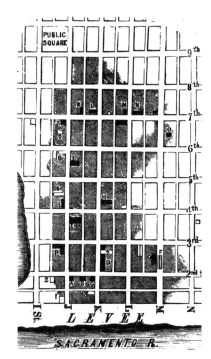

This diagram of the devastated area in the 1852 fire shows the extensive damage as well as some buildings left mysteriously standing.

Less than two years after the 1852 destruction, the flames struck again on July 13, 1854. While compared to the 1852 fire this one was not as extensive, but it was just as costly in damage.

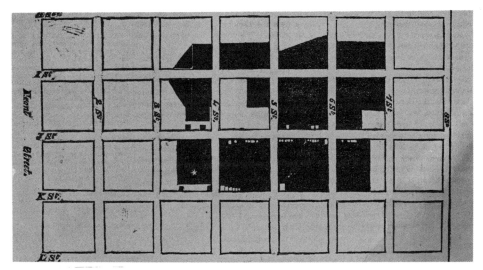

In these years, too, there was another drama in the making: the extraordinary effort, in the relatively primitive decade of the 1850s, of the raising of the city itself. It represents a fantastic enterprise. It defies the imagination of those unlettered in simple engineering to comprehend the raising of a downtown city floor, buildings, and ground—four, five, six feet, then as much as 12 feet.

Recall that Sacramento came into life on a plain known to have been awash many times. Twenty-five years before Sutter, the Indians recounted to the early settlers, there were "great waters" and all was flooded in the lowlands of the two rivers.

In planning for the city's future, Sutter had looked for higher ground and had selected an area about two miles south of the confluence of the American and the Sacramento rivers for its construction, and he planned to call it Sutterville. His son, John Sutter, Jr., and Samuel Brannan and others, had not Captain Sutter's foresight, however, and insisted on developing the city near the confluence. Of course the error in judgment was exposed quickly. In 1850 the new city experienced its first flood—a flood which was to generate a plan for the building of levees, and then to raise the city itself. It was a plan which would take nearly a quarter of a century to implement.

After the waters receded in January 1850, a levee three to five feet high was strung hastily from Sutterville to the Sacramento River, then northward around Sutter Slough to the American, and along the American to high ground. The earthen collar lulled the city into a false sense of security. In 1852, the rivers rose again, and again the entire city was left standing in a cold sludge of floodwaters.

It was agreed the levees must be improved, and they were to be improved, but the concern inspired others to plan bigger—to raise the city, buildings and all. It was to be a mammoth project bringing into play local government, private enterprise, and the cooperation of hundreds of merchants. A thesis by Barbara Lagomarsino, on file at California State University, Sacramento, brings together the scattered elements of this Herculean community undertaking. It is from that work that many of the details of that little-known piece of history are taken.

Especially in a town which grew as fast as Sacramento did, muddy streets are a definite problem. This view of 3rd and J shows one experiment at paving in which wooden planks were placed in the roadway.

The Remarkable Rise

The first suggestions to elevate the streets and the buildings themselves with jack screws were heard in 1853. The proposal was greeted with mixed feelings. A consensus developed by midyear, however, and the work began.

Most of the fill for the streets was brought in by wagon, but one enterprising contractor put down almost a half-mile of railroad track to carry the material down N to 9th and then over to J. His ambitious plan proved too slow and costly, though, and the railroad was abandoned in favor of wagons.

J was raised by about four feet; K and I a little more and a little less. The grade was carried to 6th on I and to 9th on J and K with cross streets raised as far as 8th. The unexpected higher expenses of raising store fronts to accommodate the higher street levels, along with over two hundred thousand dollars in assessments, proved a severe hardship on the merchants. But the effort was credited with helping to regain Sacramento's supremacy over the newly created wayside of Hoboken nearby and others trying to capitalize on the devastation of the flood.

Nine years of comparative meteorological calm followed, but then in December of 1861, and into January of 1862, the worst flood ever recorded struck. The devastation prompted gloomy prophets to surface as they had in 1852. The *San Francisco Morning Call* said: "It is simply an act of folly for the

After the flood of 1861–2, Sacramentans were prodded into the incredible task of raising themselves quite literally out the way of future high water. No job was too big for the ambitious crews. The courthouse, also used as a state capitol, was no exception. The town was indeed a city on stilts.

people of the town of Sacramento to endeavor to maintain their city on its present location." The *Nevada Transcript* was more succinct: "Sacramento is a doomed city."

Actually, discussions on raising the streets still more had been under way even before the latest inundation, but they produced two spirited camps: those favoring filling the streets only another two feet or so and those advocating a true high-grade effort of eight feet or more. All agreed levee improvement was necessary.

The supervisors previously had established a high water mark, known as Hite's grade for the supervisor who suggested it, of 22½ feet above the river bottom. Druggist R. H. McDonald, a businessman since 1849, vigorously promoted a substantial elevation of at least seven feet and attempted to promote the idea by claiming the basements thus created would add more value to the property than the cost of creating them. But official governmental action was absent in 1862 as the supervisors studied the situation.

A plan for street grading was beginning to accelerate by early 1863 but opponents claimed the public was not behind it. Coincidentally, an election was at hand which was to become a sort of referendum on the issue. The combined city-county government established in 1858 was coming to an end and three trustees were to be elected to administer the city. The results put H. T. Holmes and Josiah Johnson, two supporters of high grading, and C. H. Swift, into the roles of trustees. By midsummer a street grading program was under way, even though it failed to conform to previously established standards of a true high grade.

A year later, one of the high-grade advocates, Johnson, had to stand for re-election. High grade became a paramount issue and Johnson won by a substantial margin. One week after the election, high grading work was resumed as the trustees let a contract to fill Front from J to M and J from Front to 2nd. Property owner J. Carolan previously had brought about the filling of Front from I to J. The cost of the new work was to range from $4.17 to $6.05 per frontage foot, depending on location. The expense of the property owner did not end there, however. He had to provide a brick bulkhead along his frontage to contain the fill, see to the raising of the 14-foot sidewalk, and raise the building itself or modify it in some appropriate way.

It was a staggering, yet necessary series of expenses, but considering the magnitude of the job a century ago, prices did not seem out of line. A home was elevated for about $500. The St. George Hotel, 160 feet long and 76 feet wide, weighing about 1,900 tons, was another matter. Yet, the entire building was lifted eight feet by 250 jack screws and dozens of men for $7,450. At the height of this activity, Sacramento was described as a city on stilts.

Literally a mountain of earth was needed for the mammoth job. Early excavations within city bounds created new problems of their own. Then, eyes were turned to the old channel of the American River, north of the Central Pacific Railroad tracks. In 1868, a new channel was cut eliminating the dangerous "S" curve in the river where it joined the Sacramento. Tons of fill material came from this region. There are descriptions of deep holes along the road. Some were as big as a city block and at least eight feet deep. Turton and Knox, prime contractors in many street and building raising jobs, owned their own 15-acre gravel pit on the Sacramento Valley Rail Road at 45th and R. Still more gravel was brought in from the Folsom area.

There were problems with street raising efforts even as it progressed. The fill had to be left months, usually over one winter, to settle. Teamsters needed all their skill to negotiate the elevated roadways and to take the ups and downs of incomplete sections of the project. Pedestrians faced perils on sidewalks which were sometimes raised in front of one store and remained at the old level at the next. Crude stairways or ramps were the means of getting from one level to the other.

The *Overland Monthly* magazine for July 1870 devoted several pages to a description of Sacramento by a visitor who regarded his stay in the City of the Plain as a baneful annoyance, at best. However, even this reluctant observer had to recognize the immensity of the job undertaken by Sacramento citizens:

[Two] streets, running straight back from the river, have been, with incredible labor and expense, filled up to a higher grade. At the outer ends of these streets, many buildings, not yet raised, seem to be dropped down, as it were, into a cellar, so that their eyes are only on a level of the street. This work has entailed an immense outlay on the city, of which some notion may be formed from the fact it costs $16,900 merely to raise one building, the Courthouse, to say nothing of the grading.

But the descent from these high-grade streets to the common level of the city is not always elegantly and felicitously effected, especially in the night. Various isolated buildings near these streets have lifted themselves up, and have a piece of pavement several feet higher than other people's. Everybody here in Sacramento builds his pavement on a different level from that of his neighbor, if possible, and does not always drive down his nails well. Consequently there are innumerable little shoulders or steps which are so exquisitely unexpected that you drop off with one foot, and plump down with the prettiest possible little nod, and a "thank'ee." Add to this that there is no gas, except on the two favored streets, and there is a large aggregation of probabilities that you will get hopelessly wrong end up.

It is generally agreed that this photograph shows the curious process of putting down Nicholson paving on J Street. It was a complicated process, described in the text, but was apparently kind to hooves.

Once the fill had settled, some kind of paving had to be applied so that new ruts and gullies would not be cut by the next rain. Planking had been tried at various times since the early 1850s but this along with brick and concrete block had not proved durable enough. The first serious efforts at paving were made in the winter of 1865–66.

A patented process known as Nicolson pavement was put down on J between Front and 2nd in December. After leveling, thin planking covered with tar provided the base on which were placed vertically alternating blocks of eight- and four-inch lengths cut from four by four timbers. Salt and then gravel went into the hollows and then tar was spread over the entire top. Nicolson provided a neat, quiet surface relatively harmless to hooves and wagon wheels. It was popular for the next few years, but eventually proved to deteriorate too rapidly.

While J went the Nicolson method, K Street merchants chose cobblestone. Six- to nine-inch cobbles were placed vertically in a foot of sand, rammed down, watered, and covered with gravel. Sturdy and durable, yes, but the cobblestone had a distinct disadvantage. It was terribly dirty.

The industrious manner in which the city had tackled the seemingly insurmountable problem of rigging levees and raising the streets won the admiration of many. The threat of a new flood in 1867 gave rise to new cries for removal of the capital but this time journalistic backers were heard throughout northern California. "The day for talk of removing the capital is past," said the *California Spirit of the Times*, and the *Sutter Banner* declared: "There never was but one objection to Sacramento City, i.e. floods, and that objection, through the energy and perseverance of her citizens is removed."

The work on raising buildings and streets was nearly complete as the 1870s began—the job coming to full completion, with the raising of the level of the downtown city by some 12 feet, by 1873. It represented a fantastic feat in engineering and in community effort then; it remains one of the singular works of the city to this day.

Chapter Six

The Making of a City

THE FRONTIER CITY was not to be found tailor-made and ready for occupancy. It came not with the wave of a wand—streets, stores, hotels; government, courts, law enforcement—or with a Move In sign posted at a landscaped city gate. The city had to be built out of the things at hand and out of the things which could be shipped in. Those who came here to seek their fortune—or to lose themselves or to find themselves—had to create their own governments. They established their own courts, set up their own police and fire controls, put up their own schools and erected the stores for merchandising and the lodging so necessary to the simple creature comforts. How they did this is an adventure in itself and of more than passing historical moment.

It is a simple matter to trace the development of the first months of the city's life. In the beginning, it clustered around the fort put up by Captain Sutter, and along the riverbank. But as the city reached inland, with growth begetting new growth, soon the young city was a patchwork of homes and merchandising houses, and then arose the certain signposts of new civilization: the church and the school.

A city, in growth, is made up of many off-shoots, and some of these deserve to be more carefully examined as parts of the whole, if only briefly. Consider government.

The time came, even in the first flush of excitement over the strike in the Sierra, for the city to draft a code by which to live. The transient was giving way to the permanent. The Embarcadero was yielding to a village and the village to a city.

On April 30, 1849, village leaders met near the river, as indicated earlier. They named 11 men to a committee to recommend a form of government and to establish the environs of that government. They suggested, as boundaries, the Sierra to the east, the Coast Range to the west, and the length of the valley north and south. No crisis had arisen and so they reasoned no formal government yet was necessary. It would suffice, thought they, to create an alcalde empowered with the combined authority of a mayor and judge, and the office

In 1856 the Neptune Hose Company joined several other volunteer fire-fighting units which had been formed since as early as 1850.

113

of sheriff. The times still were relatively simple. The thief was still tried by a show of hands and he might be lashed with rawhide, perhaps 40 times, then released and banished, never to return. It was not unlike the swift dispatch of justice, with its occasional cases of miscarriage, common to frontier law elsewhere in those building years.

Perhaps this was sufficient in the beginning but in a very short time, with the rush of miners through Sacramento bound for the diggings, it did not suffice. Government, a functioning government, was needed.

Those who drafted the early documents and argued for the processes of government were exceptional men, for most who came to the new city were not concerned with government but with the new opportunity they found. They were businessmen anxious to make their fortune; and they were gamblers, anxious to take away fortunes; and they were professional men, anxious to establish practice. Most had little time for city charters and fundamental law.

There were those, however, who did look beyond the moment, into the future. Like A. M. Winn, who became the first to serve as council president. Or John Rogers and H. E. Robinson who, with others, fought to win approval for the first proposed city charter. It was aimed at creating more sophisticated law enforcement but was defeated by gambling elements which liked things wide open, unpoliced. The charter was to win in a second election, however.

By the fall of 1849, the city was operating under its locally approved charter; and this authority existed until the state legislature, in February 1850, passed an act to incorporate Sacramento City. The act also called for the election of a mayor, a recorder, and a council of nine. More than 2,500 votes were cast in the first election under that authority, and Hardin Bigelow of Michigan won overwhelmingly, polling 1,521 votes. He was to succumb to cholera that same year, however, and be succeeded by Horace Smith, who served until 1851 when James R. Hardenbergh was voted to the first of two terms.

The charter under which Sacramento was organized was amended by the legislature in 1851 to call for the division of the city into three wards with each receiving three councilmen. Other offices served not districts but the city as a whole. A harbormaster was authorized as well.

Meantime, the exploding growth brought exploding demands for city services, including water and gas. The city had both by 1854.

Those who settled early in the Sacramento Valley in the wake of the Gold Rush had two sources of reasonably potable water—the Sacramento River and a few wells. Neither was a palatable wellspring.

Upstream, miners had polluted the water to a point at which the flow was so muddy early settlers sarcastically termed it "Sacramento straight." In the early 1850s many wells were dug in search of better water but, again, the results were hardly satisfactory. The water was usually too full of iron, sulphate, and vegetable matter for taste.

Goaded by an aroused citizenry, the city launched the first municipal waterworks project—mentioned earlier—in 1853. After the voters approved the levy of a three-quarters of one per cent tax, Sacramento borrowed $284,495 under bond obligation to finance the water distribution program, and created the post of water superintendent at an annual salary of $3,000. The price of

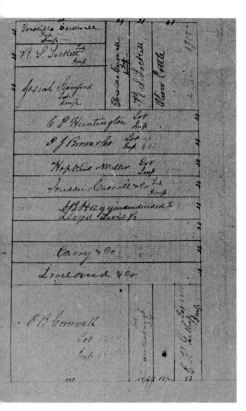

Some names which were to become famous—Stanford, Huntington, Hopkins—appear on the 1852 tax assessment books. K Street runs along the left side and 3rd is the intersection at the top of this block.

water to families not exceeding eight people was two dollars per month.

Coleville's *Sacramento City Directory* for 1854 praised the establishment of the City Water Works in glowing terms, some of which are excerpted:

To Sacramento belongs the honorable distinction of having erected the first edifice and machinery in California for supplying her citizens and the Fire Department with water. In the very midst of her afflictions, the project was conceived, when as yet, large portions of her corporate limits presented the sad spectacle of eligible building lots, covered only with the ruins of conflagration.

The site of the City Water Works is a narrow point of land, bounded on the west by Front Street, on the north and east by Sutter Lake, and on the south by I Street.... [The structure embraces] an area of 50 by 125 feet, on which were erected firmly knit brick walls, 35 feet in height, surmounted by the principal reservoir from which the city draws its supplies, with capacity for 240,000 gallons of water, and a fall of 40 feet to the grade of J Street.

In 1854, the city began construction of the Gas Works. It was a "gasometer tank" 56 feet and 6 inches in diameter. The foundation was piled and doubly capped with heavy timbers upon which was laid a covering of concrete, stone, sand, and cement. Above the works rose a chimney of 85 feet, described in contemporary accounts as a "fine specimen of masonry."

And just as the city had to be resourceful in establishing these utilities, it was plagued, as well, by sewage disposal problems. Of all of the problems which faced the young city, perhaps none was more exasperating, for it was a problem which was to persist for generations.

The first attempts at disposal were the most obvious—cesspools, septic tanks, drainage ditches. Thompson & West's *History of Sacramento County* says:

"During high water each year water would seep in through the earth and make unpleasant pools, which would remain standing until evaporated or absorbed by the earth. Pumps were tried, but with meager success."

By 1864 the problem had become so acute the Sacramento Drainage Canal was built to carry off sanitary sewage and storm drainage. It began at 6th and R streets where all the sewage of the city was discharged. From this point to Y Street, it consisted of a cement pipe 30 inches in diameter. The canal became an open ditch on Sutterville Road, at which now is the southwest corner of the Land Park Zoo, and continued south to an outlet at Snodgrass Slough about 23 miles south. In the city, main sewers were laid gradually, running north to south with connecting east-west lines. All eventually terminated at the 6th and R streets canal outlet.

Problems of Population

What kind of economy could the city depend upon in those years? In 1852, there were 100,000 miners in the Sierra, and the harvest in gold that year was $45 million. In 1853, the take was $56 million. By 1854, the number of miners had decreased somewhat, to 86,000, but the take was even greater, some $61 million.

Despite the prosperity, Sacramento's city indebtedness increased. The

The Early Economic State

thought was advanced that there would be a saving if the city and the county governments were to consolidate. One proposal suggested that the county be divided into two entities, one embodying the city and the other the lands outside the city. The consolidation proposal which was passed in 1858 rejected this premise, however, bringing under one government and one authority all lands in the county. It was a proposal fought hard by the smaller towns, such as Folsom, and the rural elements.

The consolidation wiped out the city council and authority for government was assumed by the board of supervisors. The board was expanded to a president who served as mayor and eight members elected to two-year terms.

The critics of this novel government would not be quieted and for the next five years consolidation was the most crucial issue in debate, ranking only with the Civil War in its bitterness. By 1863 the opposition had become so organized that the legislature responded and approved a new charter abolishing the consolidated government and setting up a five-man board of supervisors to govern the county. The charter established a new city government of three trustees: one was ex officio mayor; a second trustee was street commissioner; and the third was superintendent of the Water Works. Terms of the charter permitted the election of an auditor, assessor, collector, police judge, and others as the board might create.

What was the makeup of the city in the building years?

In 1856, to take a year of some fulfilled maturity, Sacramento had some seven million dollars of taxable property on the rolls. There were, within its corporate limits, about 500 brick and 2,000 frame buildings—the overwhelming number of which had been built since the 1852 fire. The city had some 30 brick yards at work producing a quarter of a million bricks a day. There were,

Gas lights glowed in the city for the first time on December 17, 1855, with the fuel being supplied from the Gas Works on Front Street.

within the city, two major lumbering mills; together they were processing about five million board feet of lumber a year.

There were six steam flouring mills operating, producing some 585 barrels of flour a day. Sacramento had two iron and brass foundries; five breweries with a capacity of 8,000 gallons per week; four soda water manufacturers capable of turning out 17,400 bottles a day; a steam factory for the manufacture of adamantine candles; a pottery works for the manufacture of earthenware and earthen pipe for irrigation; two soap factories; a salmon fishery. On and on reads the directory.

Moreover, there were, to give a quick profile of the agricultural scene, 47,305 acres under cultivation in the county; there were 70,218 apple trees under harvest and some 137,000 peach and 28,700 pear trees under cultivation to name only three fruit crops.

There were, in a year, 611,000 bushels of grain ground, valued at $916,000; and Sacramento was served with 10 toll bridges, one railroad with 22 miles of track—California's first railroad, the Sacramento Valley Rail Road, which operated between Sacramento and Folsom. In 1857 some 23,255 animals were slaughtered for meat, valued at $327,170. The count revealed the area had 43,520 chickens, 12,924 sheep, 736 goats, 8,115 hogs, 5,593 horses tamed for use, and 1,102 mules. And, oh yes, there were three asses.

California's first water distribution system rose in 1854 at the corner of Front and I Streets. A 240,000-gallon reservoir supplied families for $2.00 a month.

Law on the Frontier

The establishment of law and order was one of the most difficult challenges facing the building city. In the Sutter years, Captain Sutter was judge, jury, and executioner. His authority was supreme. In the gold years, one-man justice no longer sufficed. Not even the alcalde rule was satisfactory. When the waves of migration began to hit the young city, there was need to establish new authority.

When A. M. Winn was named unofficial mayor, in 1849, N. C. Cunningham was appointed to the post of city marshal. Little is known of Cunningham but when the first city election was held in April 1850, he won the job officially and became the city's first elected town marshal. Police responsibility for the city was to rest in this office until 1863, when the new charter providing for the end of consolidation also would make provision for creation of the office of chief of police.

The administration of justice fell under the jurisdiction of the county, and in the April election, 1850, E. J. Willis was elected the first judge of Sacramento County, while the key post of county sheriff went to a dashing young figure who seems to have had all those qualities of the legendary town tamer. He was young, in his early twenties, and, say accounts circa 1850, "handsome and brave." The first sheriff: Joseph McKinney. And, as if to add to his almost fictional recommendations, he was the operator of one of Sacramento's numerous gambling halls, the Gem.

(The chronicle of the Squatter Riot and subsequent events are to be found elsewhere, but it is part of this story to recount that McKinney fell before a hail of bullets during pursuit of squatters at Brighton.)

City Marshal Cunningham's name is strangely absent from accounts of

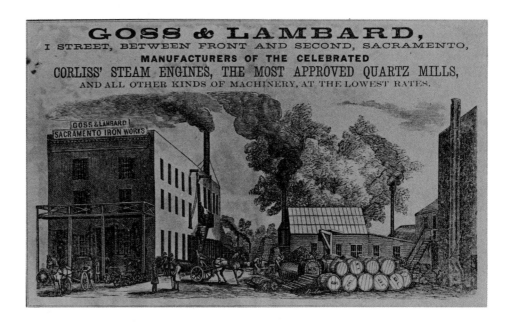

Before the first decade ended in Sacramento, Goss and Lambard's Iron Works was among the largest employers in the city. The demand for something more than the basics of food and clothing gave rise to industry such as this, which provided machinery for the mining and agriculture districts.

the squatter troubles. Indeed, City Recorder B. F. Washington was appointed marshal after the gunfire at 4th and J which left several dead and Mayor Bigelow wounded. Washington and his newly appointed deputy marshal, Captain J. Sherwood, are credited with bravery during the crisis. Ben McCullough was named sheriff after the death of McKinney, and held the job until the election the following year.

Keystone of the legal structure in the early days was the county court of sessions, a three-member panel which sat in judgment in criminal matters. It was composed of the county judge, who was elected, and two associates who were selected from among their own number by a convention of the various justices of the peace. Sacramento's court of sessions came into being May 20, 1850, when C. C. Sackett and Charles H. Swift were named associates to join Judge E. J. Willis on the tribunal.

Those who occupied county offices are too numerous to list here but it is interesting to note the turnover during the first two decades. Either by their own choice or the voters' choice, most did not succeed themselves. No sheriff held his post for more than a single two-year term until 1875. The county judge held his job a little longer. Judge Willis managed two terms before being replaced by John Heard in 1853. Robert Robinson took over four years later.

Some of the city marshals displayed greater longevity in office. W. S. White who was elected in 1851 after Washington served out the term of Cunningham, was replaced by David McDowell in 1852, but came back for two one-year terms in 1853-54. Then came men named Haines, McAlpin, Lansing, and Hardy, before J. J. Watson became marshal for four years beginning in 1859.

When the charter was changed in 1863, the form of government was altered as well. The chief of police became, as was said, the chief law enforcement officer. J. T. Clark was Sacramento's first chief of police, but he was removed after only a few months' service and was replaced by D. H. Lowry. In

1864, F. T. Burke took over the police department for four years, followed by B. W. Martz and George Smith for terms of two years each.

Throughout the early years, the city was relatively free of incidents wherein townspeople, frustrated by ineffectual authority, took matters into their own hands. But, here as elsewhere, there were exceptions. San Francisco, where the Vigilance Committee rose and submerged and rose again throughout the 1850's, was held up by the more impatient as an example of how law should be handled. In 1850, N. C. Cunningham, the first city marshal of Sacramento, tried to prevent a mob from executing violent justice on a gambler named Roe who had gunned down a merchant named Meyers while the latter was trying to break up a fist fight, but Cunningham failed. After a hasty trial, without benefit of defense attorney and with some 2,500 angry men goading them on, a so-called jury found Roe guilty. This sent the mob careening to the jail at 2nd and J. They tore out awning posts and used them as battering rams to break in the door. They overcame Deputy Sheriff Harris, who held them off for some time with the aid of a small posse, and dragged Roe to a large oak on 6th between K and L. There Roe was hanged. Lynch law had been introduced to the City of the Plain.

The following year, 213 Sacramentans emulated their brothers in San Francisco and officially formed a Vigilance Committee. It lacked the cohesion and longevity of the Bay group, but apparently was responsible for at least one incident of rope justice.

Four men were convicted of robbing and beating a citizen, a crime often punishable by death in early California. They were properly tried and convicted, but while a throng stood by at 4th and O to witness the executions, word came that one had been reprieved by the governor. Members of the Vigilance Committee, angry, balked at turning the man loose. They surrounded the reprieved prisoner and after the other three were hanged, hanged the pardoned man with chants of approval from several thousand onlookers.

Afterward, the committee attempted to get legal blessing, ex post facto, for the execution during a meeting in the Orleans Hotel. They charged that the Governor was guilty of unnecessary interference and called for him to resign. He refused. Soon the Vigilance Committee fell from favor and never did it rise in authority again.

As Sacramentans organized to protect themselves against crime, so did they turn to the task of protecting themselves, as best they could, from still another scourge of frontier life, fire. Sacramento's structures were particularly vulnerable, as emphasized earlier. Made of canvas and clapboard, they were prey to the hazards of chimney waste, the kerosene lamp, the open flame. Even before the hundred thousand dollar fire scorched Front Street in April, 1850, Sacramentans began to agitate for some kind of organized fire protection. The *Placer Times* reported the concern. It argued that not only was the city vulnerable to fire, but there were no cisterns which might be used to fight fire.

On February 5, 1850, concerned Sacramentans met at the City Hotel and produced California's first organized volunteer fire company, the Mutual

The Great Volunteers

First In Danger and Always Ready

The inscription above appears amid the ornamentation on the silver trumpet on the next page. The elegance of the instrument testifies to the sophistication the volunteer companies had reached in 1853, when the horn was a gift to Unit Foreman George B. Gammons of Engine Company Number 3. The man at left holds a similar trumpet; they could be heard for a mile, summoning volunteers.

Since almost every city, especially those associated with the quick rush of mining operations, was started as a town of tents and wooden structures, fire was a constant threat. And practically every city was at some time destroyed in part or entirely by fire. Some vanished after one or more holocausts.

But Sacramento was able to organize a number of volunteer companies and fight back. These companies, like the Neptune, the Young America, and the Alert, were dotted around the city and put an effective check on the kinds of fires which swept through in 1852 and 1854.

Three of Sacramento's fire fighting companies appear in all their splendor from left to right: Engine House Number 3, Alert Hook and Ladder, and Fire House Number 1.

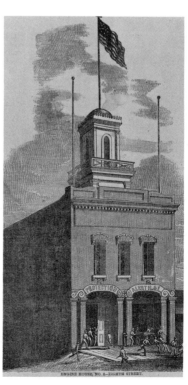

The Young America Engine Number 6 fire house on 10th between I and J is shown in a photograph at left and in an artist's rendering above. The man in the center foreground of the photograph looks like he might have been in charge of the hose inspection that day.

"In a single night our beautiful city has been swept away by the terrible element with which we are accustomed to associate the end of all earthly things." So said the *Sacramento State Journal* under the headlines below on November 12, 1852. This was a "steamer edition," published by many newspapers to report events to those in the East.

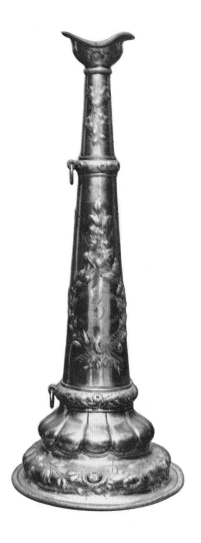

Sacramento State Journal Extra---For the Atlantic States, by the Golden Gate.

AWFUL CONFLAGRATION.

SACRAMENTO CITY BURNED TO THE GROUND.

Ten Millions of Dollars worth of Property totally destroyed!

LOSS OF LIFE.

This was one of the warnings published to remind early Sacramentans of the danger of fire.

Hook and Ladder Company No. 1. It was on hand when Front Street burst into flames in April, and it used a borrowed rig belonging to Lewis and Bailey, merchants.

On March 10, 1851, a Citizens Fire Committee was formed, and it collected some $7,000 in subscriptions to purchase more equipment and to place seven cisterns on J and K from which water could be pumped in the event of fire.

Confidence Engine Company No. 1 was organized in March, 1851, and eventually shared with Mutual No. 1 a handsome building on the east side of Third between I and J. Two other companies were organized that same year: Protection Engine Company No. 2 and Sacramento Engine Company No. 3, and the Mutuals reorganized.

The Alert Hook and Ladder Company joined the ranks of the volunteers in September, 1852. Two more took to the streets in 1853: The Tehama Hose Company No. 1 and the Eureka Engine Company No. 4. These were joined a year later by the Knickerbocker Engine Company No. 5.

The age of volunteer fire companies was colorful, exciting. There was great *esprit de corps* among members of the volunteer units, and great competition. They entertained sumptuously. Banquets, balls and benefits were common.

While manpower was strictly volunteer the city did provide leadership through an appointed chief engineer. Hiram Arents was the first to get the job. Eventually the companies were equipped, and well, by the city which also created impressive buildings to house them.

Young America No. 6 joined the list of fire fighters in 1856, as did the Neptune Hose Company. In 1860, the Broderick Engine Company No. 7 came along; and there were several others which were short lived. The important thing is that these companies created the citizen fire fighting front so necessary to that period. After the devastation of the 1852 and 1854 fires, the volunteers performed an essential service in keeping fires manageable.

But the city continued to grow. The competitive rivalry and occasional animosity which inevitably came to plague the companies sometimes seemed to get in the way of the main effort of fighting fires.

So it was in 1872 that the legislature would create a professional fire department in Sacramento. Fifty thousand dollars in bonds would be authorized and a board of fire commissioners set up.

Thus, the end was written to a dramatic episode of Sacramento's growth. When the city's fire fighting organization was professionalized, greater efficiency may have been created but something passed out of the romance that was Sacramento.

The Community Comes Together

Sacramento was a frontier town for an amazingly short period. The wild and the lawless and the vulgar gave way, shortly, to the orderly and the established. Behind the rough exterior, Sacramento society was making headway toward a certain sophistication as early as 1849. For example, a sumptuous banquet and public reception was given in the city for Gen. P. F. Smith, military commander on the coast; Commodore Jones, in command of the navy; and Thomas Butler King, a federal civilian representative. It called forth all the refinements that could be found as Captain Sutter, Sam Brannan, B. F. Gillespie, and W. R. Grimshaw, along with others, did their best to impress the guests.

On the Fourth of July in 1849, a grand ball was given in the City Hotel. Again, propriety was the watchword; the surrounding country was combed to locate women who might grace the ball as guests. Eighteen showed up, apparently easing the pain of the $32 admission charge for ticket holders.

Wherever the place or whatever the period of history, men thrown together reach out, in their common bond, to touch fingers. So was it in early Sacramento. Even before the Gold Rush, the diaries of John Sutter reveal his greatest enjoyment was to entertain, to host grand dinners. With the Gold Rush, there came the inevitable—the creation of fraternal and social orders.

Consider now, the organization, in early Sacramento, of some of the early fraternal and social orders. To begin, the organization of the Free and Accepted Order of Masons.

Preliminary meetings in 1849 led to the organization on January 8, 1850, of a Free and Accepted Masonic Lodge. A traveler to Sacramento, a Mason, had with him a charter issued to Connecticut Lodge No. 75, and he offered its use for organization of a lodge here. Thus, it took the name Connecticut Lodge. It was eventually changed to Tehama Lodge No. 3.

The Masons met in the old Red House at 5th and J in which the Grand Lodge of California, incidentally, was organized on April 19, 1850. But the Masons moved from the quarters to new meeting rooms in the old Market House on M near 2nd when the downstairs rooms of the old Red House were let out by the landowner for "immoral purposes." There is no specification of the "immorality" involved—it could have been gambling; it could have been women practicing the oldest profession in the world. Regardless, the Masons moved.

Freemasonry beckoned to those of other races and as early as 1853, early Negro settlers organized the Philomathean Lodge No. 2 F. & A. M. (Colored).

The Independent Order of Odd Fellows was introduced to Sacramento in August, 1849, by A. M. Winn, first mayor and organizer supreme, who was to be a prime force behind the organization of the Native Sons of the Golden West in 1875. He was a member in good standing both of the Odd Fellows and the Masons and brought both fraternal groups into play in efforts to aid new arrivals ill and weakened by long journeys.

The I.O.O.F. and the Masons distinguished themselves during the cholera plague of 1850 giving aid and nursing the afflicted. Later, the Masons and Odd Fellows together erected a joint hospital.

The I.O.O.F. Auxiliary, known as the Rebekah Lodge, apparently was the first such organization for the women in the city. Rising Star Lodge No. 8 was formed at the end of 1871 with 71 members.

The Jewish community in Sacramento, an active entity from very early times, organized a chapter of the Hebrew Benevolent Association in 1850. It became incorporated in 1854, the same year in which the Sacramento Turn Verein was organized. The Turn Verein, an organization of German descend-

In 1854, a portion of A. A. Bennett's spacious building on J between Front and 2nd was the Masonic Hall.

Fraternal orders appeared early in Sacramento's history. A. M. Winn, a man of vast civic energies, had belonged to the Masons and Odd Fellows before traveling West. The Odd Fellows met on the third floor of the Madux Building at 3rd and K.

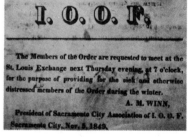

ents still noted for its glee club, built a hall in 1859 on K between 9th and 10th.

The Young Men's Christian Association has had an organization in Sacramento since 1866.

There were other social and fraternal groups in the city over these years. Among them, the Independent Order of Good Templars began its Sylvan Lodge No. 2 in 1856. The Sacramento Grange No. 12, Patrons of Husbandry, was organized in 1867. The Independent Order of Red Men was active in the city from 1867 when its Cosumnes Tribe No. 14 was formed. This was followed in 1869 by the Red Jacket Tribe, and in 1871 by the Owasso and Red Cloud Tribes.

The many social functions of such organizations coupled with the thriving entertainment business of Sacramento theater gave the city a full-fledged society in its early years. Part of the inspiration was to create social outlets, the like of which they had left behind to journey to California.

Into whatever new territory the human race extends its influence, religion has not been far behind and in many cases, as with the Spanish and Mexican expansion, the church led the way. The influences of the early church has been covered previously in this work. Their benevolent and evangelistic activities were a part of the city's beginnings. Suffice it to say that by the end of 1850, residents and transients in Sacramento had a broad choice of places to worship.

The First Church of Christ (Congregational) probably was the leader from the earliest months due to its lack of emphasis on denominationalism and its dynamic pastor, the Rev. Joseph A. Benton, who continued as the city's prime religious leader for many years.

His was not the only successful early church, however. There was the Methodist Episcopal Church which had three branches even in those early days. The Methodist Episcopal Church at 7th and L was the first to organize, but was quickly followed by a Methodist Episcopalian Church organized by Negroes three blocks north. A little later, a Methodist Episcopalian Church, South, was put up on 7th between J and K. The Grace Protestant Episcopal Congregation was among the earliest to meet, and in 1850 built on 8th between

Early churches included, from left to right: St. Mary's; the entrance gateway, chapel, and cemetery lodge; the Episcopal Grace Church; and the Congregational Church.

I and J. The First Baptist Church was organized in mid-1850, after an initial attempt in November of 1849. They built their place of worship on 4th between K and L.

The First Presbyterian Church was organized in 1856 and began meeting in Philharmonic Hall on 6th between J and K. Attempts to raise money to buy the hall failed and the church was dissolved in 1863. On January 21, 1866, Westminster Presbyterian Church was organized and a place of worship was built at 6th and L.

Sacramento's religious history is different from that of the coastal communities founded by Spain and Mexico. There, the Roman Catholic Church dominated from the beginning due to its position as the state church. But in the City of the Plain all faiths were housed because the migrants were of all faiths.

St. Rose of Lima, of the Catholic faith, was organized in 1850 but its impressive bell tower did not rise at 7th and K until 1854; and it was not until 1859 that its one-ton bell, which was to become so familiar, rang out for the first time.

Sacramento had an active Jewish community from its earliest settlement. Those of the Hebrew faith found a place for worship within the Hebrew Benevolent Society, referred to earlier and organized in 1850. It met in various places in the early years; it was not until 1859, when it acquired the old Methodist Episcopal Church on 7th between L and M, that it had its own quarters, however. The society was to play an influential part in Sacramento's early life, and was to win the respect of the community for its selfless ministrations to the needy and to the ill.

Thus did the church come to the high-spirited city. Certainly the presence of a special conscience, as embodied in worship, had a civilizing influence on the city gold built.

A Flourish of Newspapers

The story of the introduction of newspapers to interior California begins now with the *Placer Times*, established at Sutter's Fort April 28, 1849, and the *Sacramento Transcript*, which began publishing one year later, on April 1, 1850. The two newspapers ushered in an era of editorial competition which saw upward of 60 journals of varying longevity appear, most to die, during the first eight years of the city's life. Of those begun in that period only two—the *Sacramento Union* and the *Sacramento Bee*—still publish.

The third newspaper to appear on the scene was launched in print October 30, 1850. It took the name *Settlers and Miners Tribune*, and was dedicated to settlers' rights in the new city, speaking out strongly against land monopolists. It was organized by Dr. C. L. Robinson, L. M. Booth, and James McClatchy.

Late in 1850, the Sacramento *Index* became the first afternoon newspaper to publish in the interior, as well as the first Whig journal introduced to the city. Edward Kemble, who started the *Placer Times* and later compiled a history of California newspapers, attributed the early demise of the *Index*, at least in part, to its condemnation of a public lynching.

The *Daily Union* appeared on March 19, 1851, almost a year after it was proposed by four *Transcript* printers involved in a labor dispute. The delay was caused by inability to secure materials necessary for publication. Dr. J. F. Morse was employed as editor by the owners who, by the time of publication, had expanded from the original four to perhaps ten partners, incorporated under the name of C. L. Hansicker and Company. The ownership changed throughout the next year, becoming E. G. Jefferis and Company. In 1853 James Anthony came into part ownership of the *Union* under a company bearing his name along with H. M. Larkin, P. Morrill and W. J. Keating. The J. Anthony Company, with partnership changing from time to time, operated the *Union* until 1875 when it was combined with another paper to become the *Daily Record Union*.

The pioneering newspapers, the *Times* and the *Transcript*, ended a fierce rivalry on June 16, 1851, when they merged in something of a shotgun wedding. Their battles had triggered a reduction in advertising rates, below cost in some instances, and when the lucrative state printing contract went to G. K. Fitch of the *Transcript*, it was not long before the *Transcript* absorbed the *Times* in a publication known as the *Placer Times and Transcript*. This larger newspaper —it measured 23 by 35 inches to the page—soon fell before the challenge of another paper with similar political views. It ended its Sacramento publication a year later, moving to San Francisco.

It was the *Democratic State Journal* which brought about the departure of the *Times* and *Transcript* and touched off a significant if somewhat irregular succession of new newspapers. To recapitulate:

Samuel J. May and James McClatchy were involved in a firm which began publishing the *Californian* in November, 1852, some ten months after the *Democratic State Journal* was started. By July, 1853, the *Californian* bought out the *Journal*, but retained the latter's name for the remainder of its existence. Then in 1855, May became editor of the *State Tribune* which he eventually owned outright. This journal withstood a battle with a paper using the same name and put out by Farwell and Company; it continued in publication until June, 1856. May's next move was to organize the *California American* with James Allen and J. R. Ridge; it was published out of the old *State Tribune* offices. The *California American* lasted until February, 1857, when May and Ridge shared direction of a new publication called the *Daily Bee*, owned by L. P. Davis, L. C. Chandler, John Church, and W. H. Tobey. James McClatchy, an associate with the publication from its origin, became chief editor by early summer. In his career in Sacramento journalism, dating from his association with the *Placer Times* in 1850, McClatchy had served as editor or writer with six early Sacramento publications: the *Placer Times*, the Sacramento *Transcript*, the *Settlers and Miners Tribune*, the *Californian*, the *Daily Democratic State Journal*, and the *Daily Times*.

The list of Sacramento newspapers, through the building years, runs too long for this accounting. But they do include the *Pacific Banner*, a Baptist organ and the first religious paper in the city; the *California Farmer and Journal of Useful Sciences*, published by Warren and Son, the prominent Sacramento feed and seed merchants (it began in San Francisco, moved to Sacramento in 1855, then returned to the Bay); the *Spirit of the Age*, later the *Sacramento Age*, a short-lived but beautifully printed journal put out in 1855 by J. A. Mitchell and George

Holbrook Baker, the artist; the *City Item*; the *Chinese News*, the city's only foreign language paper which lasted about two years beginning in 1856; the *Phoenix*, described by Edward Kemble as "being a vehicle for the malignant abuse and indecency of a private individual," which lasted only a few months, with the final editions under the masthead *Ubiquitous*; and many, many more.

Recalling the boisterous early years, when attention was riveted almost exclusively upon the business of making fortunes, and when life had a transient character, it is small wonder the lamp of learning in Sacramento was slow to take flame.

The issue of schools and the responsibility to provide education prominently occupied the writing of the State Constitution in 1849, but implementation remained largely conversational for the next five years. So an attempt, meantime, was made to fill the breach with private schools.

In August 1849, C. T. H. Palmer rented a building on I at the corner of 3rd owned by a Professor F. Shephard and there sought to establish a school. It lasted one month, attracting no more than ten students on its best days.

The school house was far from inviting. Palmer furnished it as best he could and after his failure, the Rev. J. A. Benton of the Congregational Church bought his equipment and tried to carry on. Benton described the building in this manner: "The structure was a one-story house, about 14 x 28 feet, covered at the ends with rough clapboards and the roof and sides were covered with old sails from craft tied up at the bank of the river. Some 'shakes' and 'pickets' were nailed over the places not covered by a piece of canvas fastened at the top and dropping before the opening. There was no floor but the ground and that was by no means level. The school-house stood on the brink of the slough, or 'Lake Sutter,' near the northeast corner of Third and I Streets."

Educating a Community

James Stratton founded his private Sacramento Academy in 1853 and in less than a year added the Female Institute. Monthly rates were given, such as Common English Branches at $6.00. Board and tuition were $250.00 for a 24-week session. One room of the building was later used as the first high school in the area.

Children of the Protestant Orphan Asylum posed about 1900 in front of the building bounded by 18th and 19th, K and L. The building went up in 1869. Sacramento High School and Sutter Junior High School have also occupied this site.

Benton's school first attracted only four students, and by his own description never exceeded a dozen before he was forced to close, due to weather and meager finances, December 1, 1849. I Street at that time was not passable for wagons.

A state school law of 1851 provided for a supervising school committee in each city, but an attempt at a common school in Sacramento failed. Another law in 1852 gave cities control over schools within their boundaries but if the municipal authorities did not act, the county assessor was to have charge as an ex officio superintendent. Still enthusiasm was lacking; so was action.

By 1853, another law provided for the assessor, at that time H. J. Bidleman, to appoint a board of school commissioners for the city. He did: Dr. H. W. Harkness, G. J. Phelan, and George Wiggins were named to that board.

The editors of the city's active journalistic fraternity took up the subject and were harshly critical of the young city for neglecting public education.

Finally, in 1854, five years after the city had successfully supported gambling halls, theaters and saloons, the board of commissioners announced that on February 20, a public school house would open on the southeast corner of 5th and K. G. H. Peck took charge of the boys (or as often was the case, young men), and a Miss Griswold taught the "female department."

Times had changed since the discouraging experiences of Palmer and Benton. Fifty boys and forty girls turned out that opening morning. In four days, enrollment increased to 90 boys and 70 girls, and within the first week the school came upon the familiar problem of overcrowding. It was not long before enrollment totaled some 200, and a second school was opened in a building called the Indiana House on I near 10th. In rapid succession, schools were established at 10th and G, 7th and K and in June, 1854, the first primary school opened in the rear of the 5th Street school.

By July of 1854, it is said that over 500 students were attending schools, public and private, with over half of them in the public schools.

By January 2, 1855, less than a year after public education was introduced to the city, the first building erected expressly as a school house was dedicated at 10th and H. It was built in fifteen days for $1,487. Shortly, Dr. Harkness reported that Sacramento could boast of six public schools with accommodations for 414 pupils but an attendance which averaged 463. Applications totaled some 110 more than that figure.

Monetary problems plagued the schools from the start. In April of 1855, Francis Tukey replaced Dr. Harkness as superintendent, and the Lee and Marshall Circus performed a benefit which netted the schools $321.

Instruction in high school subjects dated from May 22, 1855, when Dr. Hatch, a board member, called for teaching in Wilson's history, astronomy, bookkeeping, and foreign languages. But classes in these subjects apparently did not begin until the next year in the school on M Street between 8th and 9th. Even so, the introduction of high school instruction gave Sacramento another distinction. It was the first or second public school of its kind in California.

The Franklin Grammar School was completed in 1858 at a cost of $7,500. Later the Washington School at 13th and G was constructed for $3,800. By the end of 1859, the city offered ten schools serving over 1,000 scholars with an average attendance of 790. The teaching staff numbered 15.

By 1872, as the city basked in the pride of a new capitol for the state, it completed its greatest monument to education to that time: The Sacramento Grammar School Building went up at 15th and J at a cost of $62,000. The multi-story structure contained 15 rooms. The student body of the Franklin School transferred there the following year.

Even in the high adventure of the Gold Rush, the young city felt the need for establishing some sort of public library. But it was not until October 1857 that enterprising citizens organized the Sacramento Library Association with a capital stock of $25,000 and offering shares at $25 each, for the establishment of a publicly supported reading room.

The capital stock was to be invested in the purchase of books, the fitting out of library rooms and the purchase, later, of a lot for construction of a permanent library. Quarters were obtained in Tukey's Building at 5th and J. Books were obtained by donation or by purchase. The library opened in November, 1857, with 800 volumes and in 1858, 800 more books were received from New York. Early reports suggest that in the beginning some 150 books were in circulation at any given time, and that the library had some 50 visitors daily.

The library moved into its own permanent quarters in 1872 on I between 7th and 8th. The handsome building cost $17,000, but some $11,000 of the amount was raised through gifts. Another milestone of culture had been passed.

One way or another, most enterprises associated with the Sacramento story began at Sutter's Fort, however primitive the beginnings might have been. Medicine is no exception. The first man mentioned in Sacramento medicine is

Medicine Comes to Sacramento

a Dr. Bates, probably Dr. Henry Bates, referred to by Captain Sutter as "the Fort physician." And about the only further record of Dr. Bates' stay came in the Sutter recollections that Dr. Bates had departed for Coloma to establish a practice in the Gold Country.

As the madness of the Gold Rush began to become epidemic in 1848, the need for doctors, drugs, and hospitals exploded with it. Many men of medicine began their Western careers in Sacramento before moving on to establish practices elsewhere. By May, 1850, 50 doctors were practicing in the burgeoning city. And there was no code of ethics to restrain them from announcing they were available. The earliest such announcement appears in the *Placer Times*, April 28, 1849. A Dr. Carpenter said he was in practice at 2nd and K and that he would be "pleased to attend to all professional calls."

The names of other physicians are to be found in the pages of the *Times*, too, but in July, 1849, a notice appeared announcing that Dr. Charles H. Cragin, formerly of Washington City, was ready to offer his professional services from an office at S. Brannan and Company. It was Cragin who was later to open the first hospital worthy of the name in an adobe building near the fort—the same building from which Brannan earlier had dispensed his wares. The doctor announced his services in the *Times* as "Sacramento Hospital . . . The subscribers beg leave to inform the public that the above larger and commodious building having been thoroughly refitted and furnished as a hospital, is now open for the reception of patients." That was on August 4, 1849. The charges were to be "as moderate as the times permit, and no sick man will be refused admission because destitute of money."

A second hospital was opened by Dr. B. Bryant that same month. His notice called attention to "A Home for the Sick . . . on L Street."

Apparently, private hospitals failed to fill the needs for on the same day of Dr. Bryant's announcement the *Times* editorially demanded a public hospital. A few days later, perhaps in response to citizen and newspaper pressure, more than fifty Odd Fellows were called together by A. M. Winn and along with several Masons effected an organization to assist those suffering from yellow fever, ague, scurvy, and intestinal disorders arising from the unbalanced diets so common among travelers. Members contributed five dollars a week for the services which were performed at the hospital of Drs. Deal and Martin inside the fort. Later, the Masons and the Odd Fellows Hospital was established by the two fraternal orders in a common and joined effort. It was located in one corner of the fort.

Other medical men were entering practice almost weekly. On December 29, 1849, Dr. J. F. Morse and Dr. J. B. D. Stillman opened a hospital at 3rd and K. These two practitioners would become lasting and influential citizens of the city and the state, and would be embraced warmly by the history they helped to write.

In the spring of 1850 the Medical Chirurgical Association of Sacramento was organized numbering perhaps 30. The Society, first medical society in California, felt physicians were providing enviable service within the city although there were stories of unreasonable gouging by some doctors.

But Sacramento's medical practice was ill-prepared for the October cholera epidemic in 1850 which threw the city into panic and brought death to great numbers—some estimates range up to 600 but a more realistic figure is the reported 364. Of whatever number dead, seventeen were physicians who refused to abandon the city as did so many citizens during the crisis. As mentioned elsewhere, the Masons and Odd Fellows performed heroically, giving both time and money—at the cost of life to many—in that crisis.

It was in the period of 1851–52 that the county established the first public hospital in the business district of the city. Dr. Johnson Price and Dr. William O. Proctor opened a hospital at Second between I and J and entered into a contract with the county for care of the poor. As it turned out, their fees were outrageously high and after three years or so the county wanted out of the agreement. A county hospital then was established at 10th and L and existed there until it was torn down in 1866. The county purchased sixty acres at a site described as "a mile south of the city limits on the upper Stockton road." It is on this site, now engulfed in the heart of the city from which it once stood so distant, that the facility, rebuilt and expanded, stands today.

The Central Pacific Railroad built its own hospital to care for its workers in 1869. Prior to this large, well equipped facility at 13th and C, railroad injuries and illnesses were cared for in a residence.

Sacramento's distinction as Camellia Capital of the World—acknowledged on all continents and enhanced by the city's annual Camellia Show and Pageant—dates almost to the city's founding.

It was the year 1852 when the city received its first camellia shipment from the Eastern seaboard. That year Warren and Company's New England Seed Store, located on J near the levee, advertised the introduction of the camellia to Sacramento life. The next year, 1853, the store published a catalog inviting the public to inspect the plant.

In its listing of the Camellia Japonica, it prophesied, "'ere long it will be acclimated with us to our pride as an ornamental tree in our gardens."

Arrangements had been made, the catalog boasted, with the "best establishments" in Europe and in the United States, for securing plantings.

The camellia was to become the city's official blossom, and through the generations certainly the city's most abundant blossom and synonymous with the city's name, Sacramento, The Camellia City.

The man who introduced the camellia to Sacramento was Colonel James Lloyd Lafayette Warren, proprietor of the New England Seed Store on J. He also was to be extremely instrumental in bringing to the city the California State Fair, for as early as 1852 he was promoting agriculture and floral exhibition—in his own store—to give Sacramento the distinction of being the first city to so display its showcase, and set the example for the state.

The state fair itself was authorized in 1854 by the state legislature. After its initial sponsorship in San Francisco, it went to Sacramento, San Jose, Stockton, and to Marysville. In 1859 and in 1860, Sacramento again won the designation; and in 1861, the state legislature permanently awarded the fair to Sacramento.

The city sponsored its first state fair in 1855 in the old state capitol at 7th

Flowers and the Fair

James Lloyd Lafayette Franklin Warren was a Massachusetts seed merchant who went West for gold and then founded the New England Seed Store on J Street. Later, he introduced the camellia to Sacramento and helped organize the state fair.

The Louisiana Race Course, a few miles south of the city, was the scene of the 1855 California State Fair. The fair was a roving exhibition in the early years, beginning in San Francisco in 1854 and later moving to San Jose, Stockton, and Marysville before returning to Sacramento. This race track was used locally in the interim.

The site of the first agricultural fair was Warren's New England Seed Store on J between Front and 2nd. Warren sponsored the event and provided the hall. The store burned in 1852, but was rebuilt and back in business in only a few weeks.

The Agricultural Hall helped attract the state fair to Sacramento. Built by the Agricultural Society, it was 160 feet square, was located at 6th and M, and took 12 weeks to build in the summer of 1859.

Though the yearly events sponsored by the Agricultural Society brought small monetary rewards, the pride of winning loving cups like this one brought some entries from far away.

Rattler, the king of the trotters at the state fair, appeared in this George H. Baker illustration in the report of the California State Agricultural Society in 1859. Competition like this brought people to town for the fair.

and I. In the years which followed, the fair was to move to four different locations: To Agricultural Hall, at 6th and M, from 1859 to 1883; to the old Agricultural Pavilion at 15th and N, 1884 to 1905; to the old State Fair Grounds on Stockton Boulevard, 1906 to 1967; and to its new, ultra-modern site near Arden on the Cal Expo Ground, 1968.

Harness racing and livestock exhibition were a part of the first fair, circa 1855. The city sponsored both as part of its fair at the old Louisiana Race Course which was located near what now is 12th Avenue and Franklin Boulevard. In its day, the Louisiana track was referred to as the "most fastionable turf in the West." In 1861, the state fair officially opened a new track in the vicinity of 20th and G; it was to be called Union Park Track.

California's First Republicans

It was in Sacramento that the Republican party in California was born. According to early reports, the first mass meeting of the new party came April 18, 1856, with E. B. Crocker, later to be associated with the Central Pacific Railroad and to be named a judge, giving the foundation address. The first GOP convention in California followed on April 30 in the Congregational Church on 6th between K and L. One hundred and twenty-five delegates from 13 counties attended—65 from Sacramento and San Francisco counties. Resolutions were adopted opposing the further extension of slave territory and slave power, welcoming immigrants, condemning attempts to prejudice immigrants against various American institutions, favoring the speedy construction of a transcontinental railroad with aid from Congress, favoring the speedy settlement of outstanding land titles, and urging the election to office of bona fide settlers only—those of some proved permanency.

The Union First

Sacramento was part of the mainstream, of course, and so when the national house began to divide over the issue of slavery and union, so was Sacramento divided. The quarrel touched every family, one way or another. No mistake, however, that Sacramento was predominantly of Union sentiment.

There is the story of an incident which happened July 4, 1861. The nation had been at war only a short time. A man carrying a large Confederate flag began to parade J Street, testifying to the Southern cause. His trek ended abruptly when a group of loyalists seized the flag and shredded it. The incident was not isolated. Confrontation was common between the Copperheads and the Loyalists, be it in living room, saloon, or newspaper.

Prior to the war, there were many Union soldiers stationed in California. Most of these were ordered to the lines when war broke out. They left a vacuum, and Sacramentans, as other Californians, were alarmed that California might be vulnerable to an attack through Texas, so a movement to organize a California Volunteer Unit produced a call for manpower enrollment in July of 1861. Some 16,000 responded; Sacramento contributed 2,000 to the force.

Local militia had been a part of the Sacramento scene almost from the city's founding, however. The first, the Sutter Rifle Corps, was organized as early as 1852, and served the city in philanthropic, ceremonial, and, occasion-

Broadsides like this one helped the new political party to some success in Civil War days because voters commonly went for a whole ticket.

CONSTITUTION

REGULAR
Union Ticket.

For State Senator,
NEWTON BOOTH.

For Assemblymen,
A. B. NIXON,   W. H. BARTON,
J. M. ENOS,   A. P. CATLIN,

The California National Guard maneuvers in the Plaza during the Civil War. Their weapon is Union Boy, an artillery piece bought by William L. Siddons to be fired after every Union victory. In the background is the William Tell House at the southeast corner of 9th and J.

ally, in military use, until it disbanded in 1857. Before it did disband, however, it had been called into service against San Francisco's Vigilance Committee—an emergency action instituted by Governor Johnson to curb the lawlessness of vigilante groups roaming the Bay City.

Meantime, the Sacramento Guards, Light Infantry, organized in 1855, was reorganized three years later as the Independent City Guard under state law. Several of their number left to serve with the Union Army. The Sacramento Hussars, inspired by colorful German cavalrymen, came into being in 1859 and was attached to the State Militia in 1863. Some of the other brightly uniformed groups helping to guard the home front were the Granite Guard of Folsom, the Washington Rifles, Sacramento Rangers, Shirland's Cavalry, the Sacramento Sharp Shooters, and the Turner Rifles. These and others gave dedication to the Union cause.

Even though 2,000 miles from the lines, Sacramento made a national impression with a substantial contribution to the Sanitary Fund, as the appeal—similar to today's Red Cross—was known. A gala railroad excursion and Sanitary Picnic was held on May 18, 1864. Some three thousand began the outing with a morning parade to the depot, led by bands and assorted military groups. There some boarded an excursion train for the ride to a pine grove in Placer County. It was a full day, but the city had opened its pocketbook well. The Sanitary Fund was $17,000 richer for the outing.

Through the war years the telegraph office on 2nd was a favorite Sacramento gathering rendezvous. There dispatches were received from the fronts, anxiously awaited and cheered or cursed, depending upon the report. The major Northern victories prompted the firing of a cannon affectionately called Union Boy—a field piece owned by W. L. Siddons—and when it was fired it was fired with pomp and ceremony.

As the end of the war neared, the gatherings at the telegraph offices grew more massive. The fall of Richmond triggered an impromptu celebration which engulfed the city. And when the telegraph key brought word the war indeed was over, the *Bee* reported the "grandest spontaneous outpouring of patriotism ever witnessed."

In one of his most famous paintings,
Charles Nahl created two moods for Sunday
Morning at the Mines, *the raucous and the serious.*

The Arts Begin

Chapter Seven

IT IS HARD to argue with a flood. The one that washed over Sacramento in January 1850 called a halt to the blossoming arts that were entertaining the Gold Rushers. The Eagle Theater, which had opened on the Embarcadero less than three months before as the first theater built in California, closed for good and the actors of Mr. Atwater's company, leaving their sets and props to float for themselves, took off for San Francisco.

But floods are short and art is long. Within months, there were five more theaters to take the Eagle's place: Lee's Exchange, the National Arena, the New Hall, the Pacific and the Tehama, which was the Eagle rebuilt and relocated. In April, Stephen Massett, the gifted English adventurer-actor-musician who had attended the Eagle's opening night with Bayard Taylor, arranged four concerts, Sacramento's first, in the New Hall at Front and M streets, featuring in the first three the elegant European pianist, Henri Herz, and in the fourth, Massett's own mixed bag of entertainment. This included songs, recitations and his "celebrated hodgeria of the YANKEE TOWN MEETING" in which he impersonated six characters.

Joseph Andrew Rowe, "the celebrated equestrian and domesticator of the horse," at 31 already a veteran of 21 years with the circus, opened his Olympic Circus in the Pacific Theater on May 2, 1850. It was such a success that three months later Sam Brannan built Rowe his own Olympic Amphitheater on the Embarcadero between K and L streets.

At the Tehama the eminent tragedian James Stark, who had studied under the great Macready in London, was offering the young city a parade of Shakespeare's most towering figures—Hamlet, Macbeth, Shylock, Othello, Richard III—as well as Benedick to the Beatrice of Sarah Kirby, later to be his wife. The appearance lasted two months; they were to return often in later years as prime favorites of an especially enthusiastic theater town.

Signora Fanny Manten, a danseuse from Milan, offered the city its first ballet program on May 22, 1850 at the Pacific Theater. The show also included a magician and ventriloquist named Signor Rossi, who held "an amusing con-

This chapter on art, music, and theater in early Sacramento was contributed by William C. Glackin, long associated with the lively arts in Sacramento.

The first theatre built in California, the Eagle, was closed by the great flood of 1850. It is shown here in a detail from the lithograph by Casselear and Bainbridge.

versation between himself and a drunken man shut up in a trunk." That same year at Lee's, Signor Llorent's troupe performed dances and selections from *Lucia di Lammermoor*.

It will be seen that the tastes of the time and place encompassed a remarkable variety. It is a bad mistake to think that because the audiences included miners fresh in from the hills, only crudity could please them. Walter Leman, whose long career in the early California theater took him everywhere in the state, later recalled: "There was an amount of intelligence in the audiences of those mining regions quite equal to that which gathered in the pit and boxes in San Francisco or Sacramento."

There was plenty of simple popular entertainment, of course, including a bullfight July 15, 1850, featuring the Mexican toreador Francisco Diez and four bulls, and, a year later, "a thrilling combat between a full sized grizzly and a large bull" which drew 2,000 on a Sunday to the Brighton race course just outside of town to the east. There were also Dr. Collyer's Living Models, whose undress delighted the miners and scandalized the straitlaced.

The worldly author Bayard Taylor, sent west by Horace Greeley, was amused at the melodrama of *The Bandit Chief* and the cockney accent of Mrs. Ray at the Eagle's opening night, and a modern theatergoer can find amusement in the very titles of the period: *The Idiot Witness, or A Tale of Blood; Six Degrees of Crime, or Wine, Women, Gaming, Theft, Murder and the Scaffold; Happy Man, or the Magic Shirt;* and *The Youth Who Never Saw A Woman.* But these were the plays Victorians elsewhere were laughing at and cheering, too. If a penchant for farce, melodrama, and spectacle can be marked in the California pioneers, they were only reflecting the tastes of their age. The custom of following a tragedy with a comic afterpiece, for instance, was an old theatrical tradition. And one name, William Shakespeare, is to be found more than any other in the newspaper accounts, handbills, programs, and memoirs of this thriving time in Sacramento theatrical history—which is to say California, since almost everybody who came to perform in the state came up the river to Sacramento.

Still, the time and place did produce an audience that was something special: generous, boisterous, adoring, and violently hostile by turns. When Catherine Hayes, brought to America by P. T. Barnum as the Swan of Erin, came to the city for the first time, the pioneers were not to be outdone by the Empire Fire Engine Company of San Francisco, which had paid a record $1,150 at auction for the first seat at her concert there. In Sacramento, the Sutter Rifles bid the price of the first reservation up to $1,200 and presented the ticket to Captain John Sutter. On the night of the concert, February 8, 1853, a picked guard of honor escorted him to a green plush sofa in the front of the Congregational Church amid a standing ovation, in which Miss Hayes joined.

On the other hand, they threw eggs at Lola Montez. We have a memorable account of the occasion from a man who shared western stages with her in 1853, a Viennese violinist named Miska Hauser, who had also been imported by P. T. Barnum. Disenchanted with Barnum's way with a dollar, Hauser took off for the West with his violin and his sense of humor intact, only mildly distressed by the fact that his audiences' favorite was a piece he had written as a joke, "The Bird in the Tree."

In San Francisco, arranging some chamber music concerts, he attracted the fancy of the internationally scandalous Lola, ex-mistress of the "mad" King Ludwig of Bavaria. Doing her best to live up to the talk of two continents, she was dancing in the theaters at night and challenging people to duels by day. To Hauser she sent flowers, for which he was subsequently billed $150. Nevertheless, he accepted an engagement to appear with her in a show in Sacramento.

For reasons Hauser does not make clear, Lola had managed to antagonize her audience in advance. When the curtain rose and she began to dance "after letting her challenging, dazzling eyes stray for a moment over the crowd," the immediate response was "uncontrolled laughter." At this Lola stopped the music.

Advancing daringly to the very edge of the stage, with pride in her bearing and fire in her eyes, she said "Ladies and Gentlemen! Lola Montez has too much respect for the people of California not to perceive that this stupid laughter comes from a few silly puppies." Renewed laughter. "I will speak!" she cried, raising her voice louder, while her eyes shot flame. "Come up here," she shouted, "give me your men's trousers and take in their place my woman's skirts; you are not worthy to be called men." Tremendous laughter. "Lola Montez is proud to be what she is, but you haven't the courage to fight with her—yes, this woman, who has no fear of you all, who despises you."

She wished to go on, but the uproar had reached its culmination point; decayed apples and eggs shot through the air and the bombardment lasted so long that this female opponent was constrained to take a better view of the male sex and with strategic backward movement withdrew herself from the firing line.

Hauser, watching from a loge seat, was dismayed when the manager

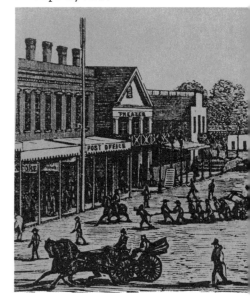

Although the Eagle enjoyed but a short life, many theaters followed. Among them was the Sacramento Theater on 3rd Street, believed to be seen here in a contemporary view.

James Stark is the professional actor credited with giving California its first performance of Hamlet, Macbeth, and several other classic roles, all in the Tehama Theater.

rushed up and begged him to improvise something to save the show. He hesitated "but the distress of the director and the six hundred dollars which he in his misery offered me for this service touched my heart and in less than five minutes I stood armed with my fiddle and bow before the hostile audience."

To his relief, they greeted him with a storm of applause. He played "The Bird in the Tree." They demanded it again, and he obliged. When shouts arose that he should continue, because "the dancer Montez is unworthy to appear before us," Lola rushed from the wings and started to dance.

"Then, like a hurricane which, in its fury, does not disdain to sweep down upon delicate flowers, the attack of the furious public upon Lola Montez began. Everyone pressed toward the stage, benches and chairs were overturned and above the martial music of crashing window panes the following battle cry was distinguishable: 'Scoundrel! We want our money back!'"

The manager hid. Hauser addressed the crowd with soothing words in broken English and then took up his violin and "played as long as I possibly could the most foolish things—"Carneval," "Yankee Doodle," "Bird In The Tree," etc., until the hall was turned from a madhouse into a theater." Hauser goes on, "Then suddenly the persevering Spaniard again appeared and in spite of the accelerated and wavering musical accompaniment, she danced the spider dance to the end. This time her perseverance won; the more wisely disposed part of the audience withdrew, but others more considerate of their dollars remained and were rewarded by the victorious dancer in divers ways."

Afterward, the malcontents gathered under her window at the Orleans Hotel to serenade her with pots and kettles. Lola's response was another furious tirade, and eventually "armed men appeared and dispersed the crowd and so there was an end of this dangerous concert."

Yet the next night, Hauser reports, the dancer, now apologetic, was greeted by wreaths tossed at her feet instead of rotten apples. When the editor of the *Daily Californian* insinuated that the enthusiasm of the crowd was due to free tickets, Lola challenged him to a duel. She offered the use either of her duelling pistols or a pair of pills, one of them poison. The duel did not occur. After five more performances she took off for Grass Valley, bought a house and settled down for two years, which is to say she kept two bears as pets, tried to horsewhip the local editor, and discovered little Lotta Crabtree, who was to become an international star of somewhat more secure position.

At eight, Lotta charmed all northern California with her singing, dancing, and comedy. She was only one of several child stars who were potent box office attractions. The Bateman Sisters—Ellen, nine, and Kate, eleven—came to Sacramento after sensational success in the east, impersonating Macbeth and Lady Macbeth, Shylock and Portia, Richard III and Richmond, in full (if miniature) regalia, complete with mustaches. Susan Robinson, eight, billed as the California Fairy Star, was the leading member of the Robinson family in 1853. At the National Theater, for "New York prices" (25 and 50 cents), she appeared "in a favorite character, also in several SONGS AND DANCES." She captivated the miners with her rendition of "Whisky in the Jug" and "Annie Laurie" and her imitation of Lola Montez doing the spider dance. Over at Rowe's Olympic Circus, Master Rafael, "the Little Rising Star," performed "daring equestrian

Feats, Leaping Whip, Garters and Hoops, riding upon his head, with the horse at full speed." There were also Master Tomasito, a contortionist, and Paul Boulbon, six, billed as the infant Paganini, to tug at the heartstrings of pioneer audiences.

Among the many famous actors to win the admiration of those audiences —and to find, in a very personal way, that the rough miners could be a kind lot—was one who was to be called the greatest actor of his time, Edwin Booth.

All of the Booths, except John Wilkes, played Sacramento. Junius Brutus Booth, Jr., was the first to come west, scouting the land for his father, who was revered as one of the age's great tragedians. Junius, Jr., began his western career in Sacramento in July, 1851 as a member of Charles R. Thorne's company at the Pacific Theater, playing Iago and Richard III. By the time the more splendid American Theater opened on September 9 he was both manager and star; the play was *All that Glitters Is Not Gold*. Two weeks later, he was off to San Francisco to take over Thomas Maguire's new Jenny Lind Theater. In less than a year he had persuaded his famous father to follow him west. Edwin, 18, came along.

Junius Brutus Booth and his youngest son Edwin sat for this portrait before touring California in 1852.

The elder Booth opened his first Sacramento engagement under his eldest son's management in the American Theater August 19, 1852, in *The Iron Chest*. Both "June" (Junius, Jr.) and Edwin were also in the cast. The newspapers, taking polite and kindly notice of the father's advancing age, were nevertheless admiring. Of Edwin, one said: "With study and experience he will yet rank among the prominent actors of the day."

In failing health, the father left for the east in October, persuading Edwin to stay in California with his brother. On November 30, on a steamer between New Orleans and Cincinnati, Junius Brutus, Sr. died.

In 1854, living with another actor in a two-room house in San Francisco, Edwin entered himself in the city directory as "comedian and ranchero." In Sacramento a year later the directory said, "Booth, Edwin, tragedian, boards Mrs. Torry's."

Sarah Kirby was James Stark's partner in the Sacramento performances. They were later married and returned to Sacramento often as favorites of the local patrons.

In his first four years in California, Edwin Booth cut his acting teeth in a remarkable variety of roles. By the time he left he was a star, but the first months were unexpectedly rugged. When the great fire of November, 1852, leveled Sacramento, June went back to San Francisco but Edwin struck out for the hills with another company as actor and banjo player. In the dead of that winter, stranded in Grass Valley, he heard the news of his father's death. Full of grief, he took off on foot for San Francisco over the objections of his friends, in the company of a group of miners who were being run out of town for a knife fight.

They made Smartsville by the first night. When the bill was presented for drinks and food, young Booth had to admit he was broke. Gulping down his sorrow, he blacked his face and played the minstrel—and a little Shakespeare— for most of the night. At Yuba Dam the next day, he collapsed. Touched, his new friends put him to bed and in the morning sent him on his way with a warm coat, gloves, and a little money.

From this arduous beginning his rise was swift. Small roles like Cassio gave way to leading parts and star billing. He played his first Hamlet ever in San

Miss Catherine Hayes stormed the American continent for P. T. Barnum, and Sacramento was on her tour. An auction for the first ticket to her 1853 concert brought $1,200 from the Sutter Rifles, and their patron, John A. Sutter, was seated with ceremony.

Strapped to a horse and wearing flesh-colored tights, Adah Isaacs Menken enthralled audiences in Mezeppa *in repeated performances without opening her mouth except to smile.*

Miss Caroline Chapman was regarded as one of America's most versatile actresses. She toured California beginning in 1853, playing comedy and tragedy until the 1870s.

Junius Brutus Booth, Jr., arrived in Sacramento in 1851 to begin a western company and play at the Pacific Theater. His presence was to lure his famous father and younger brother a year later.

143

One of the great stars of early California theater was W. B. "Uncle Billy" Chapman. Among his talents was an ability to look 20 years younger than he was, and he was taken for Caroline's brother instead of her father.

Julia Dean Hayne was a star of the New York stage playing Camille when she left to journey to the West. Arriving in Sacramento in June 1856, she was soon playing the same role in the Forrest Theater.

The Bateman children, Kate and Ellen, had earned star billing in the East before they came to booming California in 1854. They did not take children's roles, but rather made their reputations playing adult roles. Not to be limited by mere adult portrayals, they also acted as men as well as women. They played many of Shakespeare's prominent characters, such as Richard III, Shylock, Portia, and Lady Macbeth. The broadside at right shows the enthusiasm they created.

THEATRE

KING & RYER ———————— MANAGERS.

Dress Circle and Parquette......$2 00.   Pit.................$1 00.
☞ Box Office open from 10, A. M. to 2, P. M., when seats may be secured. ☜
Doors open at 7½—Performance to commence at 8 o'clock.

TRIUMPHANT SUCCESS OF THE
PRIZE DRAMA!

☞ Last Night of the Engagement of the Renowned

BATEMAN
CHILDREN!

☞ The Local Drama, for which the prize of ONE THOUSAND DOLLARS! was awarded to the successful Authoress, Mrs. SIDNEY FRANCES BATEMAN, having received the stamp of POPULAR APPROBATION in Sacramento, will be repeated this evening, for the LAST TIME, when all who would witness the Drama, which has been attended with the greatest EXCITEMENT and ENTHUSIASM ever witnessed since the establishment of the Drama in California, will have the last opportunity.

New Scenery,... by Mr. Campbell
Machinery,.. by Mr. Marsh
Music (composed and arranged expressly for this Drama,)............ by Mr. Geo. Loder
And a

Grand Moving Panorama!

Saturday Evening, Aug. 5th, 1854,

Will be presented, for the last time, the NEW PRIZE DRAMA, written by Mrs. SIDNEY FRANCES BATEMAN, entitled the

Mother's Trust!
Or, California in 1849.

Zeke Stubbins, (A Wide-awake Yankee Boy, with a Comic Song,)...Miss ELLEN BATEMAN
Ben, (The Devoted Son)...Miss KATE BATEMAN

Gilmore	Mr. RYER	Adolphus Muggins	Mr. CAMPBELL
Colcord	HAMILTON	Thompson	SMITH
Squire Merrill	KING	Vocal Joe	JAMISON
Van Snip	DUMFRIES	Cottonade Jack	CHARLES
Britten	SAMPSON	Gambler	ROGERS
Fairfax	HARROLD	Miner	DELVER
St. John	FOLLAND	2d Miner	DIGGORY
Mr. Villers	CONNOR	Emily	Miss S. EDWIN
First Mate	JONES	Mrs. Masters	Miss E. EDWIN
Gambler	PEMBERTON	Mrs. Von Snip	Mrs. CAMPBELL

Sailors, Miners, Chorus, &c.

⚫⚫⚫ PROGRAMME OF INCIDENTS. ⚫⚫⚫

Act I.—*Scene 1st*—Bar-Room of a Village Tavern in New Hampshire....The Good Fellow who is nobody's enemy but his own....The Schemer, who drinks while other men pay....Arrival of the Mail...."*Still Later from California!*"....A Yankee Trader, on a small scale....Gold the prevailing topic....The Rights of Women practically illustrated.——*Scene 2d*—Parlor in Villars House....The Belle of the Village....Arrival of old friends.... ZEKE "allers lookin' eout for the main chance!"....Agreement for a trip to California. A catalogue of necessaries.——*Scene 3d*—Gilmore's Homestead....The wife and daughters ....The Mother's Comfort....An unwelcome Guest....The proposed Sale....The agony of despair...."Could not I go with Father?"....The Father's Welfare entrusted to his Child...

Discovered by Lola Montez, Lotta Crabtree captivated audiences at the tender age of eight and became a mature actress later.

The famous Lola Montez made her place among entertainers both on and off the stage with her dances and verbal matches with audiences and anyone else who displeased her.

145

The Forrest Theater was a monument to the arts when it went up at 2nd and J in 1855. But show business always was risky, and by 1859 the building was used as a gymnasium.

Francisco April 25, 1853. He acted all over the mining country—Jackson, Columbia, Placerville, Angel's Camp, Auburn. Sacramento saw him as Hamlet, Richard III, Shylock, Othello, Iago, Malvolio, Macbeth, and as Bucket, the detective, in *Bleak House*, as Wildrake in *The Love Chase*, and Mr. Brownsmith in *Little Toddekins*, described as a comedietta. His greatest success was a remarkable run of 14 performances—perhaps unprecedented in that day and place—in *The Marble Heart*. Finally, in September 1856, he said farewell to Sacramento with Iago and to San Francisco with King Lear, and sailed for home in the east. He was to return 20 years later as the most famous actor in America to play Iago and Richard III once more, and again in 1887, six years before he died.

A Universal Theater

The Booths bore only one of the great theatrical names to be found on the playbills of the Gold Rush and the decades that followed. Almost everybody who was anybody in the American Theater in the second half of the nineteenth century came west, and almost every actor who came west played Sacramento.

The area even made its own stars, like the widely worshipped Sophie Edwin, who came to the city from her native Australia at the age of 10 and, legend has it, sold pies and cakes in a local saloon. By 1859, at 19, she was "an old Sacramentan and universal favorite" of the theater, according to a handbill from the Metropolitan Theater. She went on to a far wider fame, only to be cut off by death at 35, in San Francisco.

As previously noted, James Stark and Sarah Kirby gave the city its first look at some of Shakespeare's greatest plays as early as 1850. Three years later one of America's great theatrical families, the Chapmans, were touring northern California with young Edwin Booth in the company, playing Hamlet to Caroline Chapman's Ophelia. Caroline got the raves. Theater historian Joseph

146

Ireland had written of her "lustrous eyes, which could convey at a glance more meaning, either of mirth or sadness, than any contemporaneous female optics of the New York stage." Her father, W. B. (Uncle Billy) Chapman, so young looking he was taken for her brother, was called "the best low comedian who has ever played in this state." His low comedy, of course, included Shakespeare's clowns.

Matilda Heron, a new star from Philadelphia, later to be acclaimed in New York and London, made her first Sacramento appearance on January 30, 1854 in one of her favorite roles, Bianca in *The Tragedy of Fazio*. Julia Dean Hayne, having triumphed in New York as Camille, offered the same role in Sacramento's Forrest Theater in November, 1856. When she returned five years later, as one of the most revered stars of the American stage, the legislature tendered her a testimonial. "Graceful as a swan," was the way her cousin, the great stage star Joe Jefferson, described her.

The parade grew in the 1860s. While Lawrence Barrett and his partner as actor and manager, John McCullough, who was ranked as a tragedian second only to Edwin Booth, were climbing the heights of Shakespeare on one set of stages, Adah Isaacs Menken, on another, was climbing an Alp while strapped to the back of a horse. Her international success as Mazeppa was extended to California in the 1860s. She was a sensation, and in more ways than one a rather unusual figure. Some time before, discouraged at her efforts to become a serious actress, she had decided to heed the words of tragedian James Murdoch: "Let the audience gaze at you in a dangerous predicament but don't open your mouth except to smile." *Mazeppa* was her answer; it was a terrible melodrama, but it gave her the opportunity, in a male role, to wear flesh-colored tights. The subsequent reaction is credited with establishing the leg show in America. In San Francisco, impresario Thomas Maguire paid her the incredible sum of $500 a performance for 60 nights. Strapped to a horse charging up a treadmill for 15 hectic minutes, she earned her place in theatrical history as The Naked Lady.

Maguire himself is worth a look as a spectacular example of the theatrical producer. Actually, he was more than that, functioning also as an agent, company manager, theater owner, and tour booker. In time, he was to be called the Napolcon of California theater.

His success was a typical Gold Rush phenomenon. In New York in 1846 he had been an illiterate hack driver. He rose to gambler, then saloon keeper. In San Francisco in 1849 he opened a saloon and built a theater above it, the first in that city, called the Jenny Lind. It was one of three to bear the name. He sold the third to the city for a city hall and built another one with the money. By 1852 he owned the Pacific and the American in Sacramento and charges of monopoly were being muttered. By 1859 he had the Forrest and the Metropolitan, too. He had a knack for spotting talent and publicizing it. He brought the west its first prima donna, Elisa Biscaccianti. She was in nearly every Shakespearean play, including 20 different productions of *Hamlet*; whatever opera he could find—he had a passion for opera—and 60 performances of *Mazeppa*. He organized minstrel companies. He maintained a theatrical agent in the eastern states and sent a scout to Australia. They said he made a million. By 1880 he had lost it. He died broke, back in New York.

Many of the leading performers played at the elegant Forrest Theater.

147

Less flamboyant but equally notable among the early theatrical entrepreneurs in Sacramento was Dr. Volney Spalding, a Harvard graduate who had come west in '49. His role as a physician was important—as superintendent of the hospital, he treated the first case of cholera in the epidemic of 1850—but he also dabbled in real estate and took a role in civic affairs from the start, being one of the first city councilmen in 1850. Always interested in the theater, he bought the saloon called Lee's Exchange in 1851, remodeled it into the American Theater and opened it September 9 with *All That Glitters Is Not Gold*. As owner-manager he presented such luminaries as Charles Thorne, James Stark, the Booths, and Frank Chanfrau. Spalding's stature with the public is indicated by a benefit tendered to him early in 1852. The capacity audience included "no less than 66 ladies" and brought receipts of $2,000; 82 citizens signed a testimonial to his generosity and public service. When the American burned in the great fire of November, 1852, Dr. Spalding returned to the east, but he was back in 10 years to settle first in Virginia City and then in San Francisco, where he died in 1886.

Theater meant more than Shakespeare and melodrama in the early years; its byways included such specialized endeavors as minstrels, Chinese puppets, and ladies in tights. Variety was the key. Consider the program presented by Charles R. Thorne's company at the Pacific Theater to celebrate Independence Day in 1851: 'The National and Patriotic Drama of THE FALL OF THE ALAMO: an Irish song, a Polka Nationale, the "melo-drama" of *The Drunkard, or the Fallen Saved;* the recitation of an ode entitled *Liberty!;* the singing of *The Star Spangled Banner*; a dance and comic song, and for a finale, a farce called *Turn Out*.'

As noted before, the Stockton Minstrels played the Eagle Theater in September, 1849, even before its official opening. The first minstrel company in America had been organized only six years before. The form was to flourish past the turn of the century. The Christy Minstrels, headed by E. P. Christy, was one of the most popular of the troupes; a handbill from the Sacramento Theater in November 1854, advertises a benefit for one of its stars, Lewis Mairs, and features another, Eph Horn. There were Charley Backus and Billy Birch, known as Brudder Bones, and the king of them all, Billy Emerson, whose reign began in 1870 with the formation of Emerson's California Minstrels.

And California theater was international. In early 1849 there were 54 Chinese men and one woman in California; by 1855, there were 40,000. Theater followed them in October, 1852, with a company from China offering "numerous feats of Skill, Dexterity, Magic, Jugglery and Necromancy" as well as a Grand Tableaux and a double-jointed dwarf. They won overflow crowds and enthusiastic reviews at the American Theater. In February of 1855 the Chinese of Sacramento began a puppet theater seating 100 in the back of a gambling establishment on I Street near 5th. The puppets, elaborately costumed, were three and four feet long. The dialogue was in Chinese but Occidentals attended, too, and soon the manager was recruiting local Chinese for live theatrical performances. Their historical plays, given May 8 and 23, were probably the first amateur theatrics in Sacramento.

It was 1860 before Occidentals organized the Sacramento Dramatic Association, first as a discussion group, then as actors presenting *The Stranger* in the

Forrest Theater. The production apparently left something to be desired; some vegetables and eggs were tossed at the stage. In 1865, the group acquired as director, Albert Hart, an amateur who had been good enough to play leading roles in McKean Buchanan's company at the Metropolitan. Under him they did a series of popular plays of the day, reaching a peak of ambition with *Esther the Beautiful Queen*, which ran three nights with a cast of 120, all local.

As for the ladies in tights, Dr. Collyer's Living Models broke the ground in the first days of the Gold Rush and Adah Menken's success, extended to the East and then Europe, set the first box office records. But *The Black Crook* really set the style to stay, and in its wake Sacramento and other northern California cities were treated to two burlesque companies in 1870. Lydia Thompson and her British Blondes, a sensation in New York, sang, danced, and enacted a variety of roles, but Thomas Maguire was right on hand with a rival troupe, also called the British Blondes. There were also Mabel Santley and her Blond Burlesquers; trying to go their predecessors one better, they were arrested for indecency in San Francisco, although Sacramento had raised no official objection. They were acquitted after no less a dignitary than Charles Crocker, vice president of the Central Pacific, testified that he considered the performance quite artistic.

The records indicate that Sacramento's first concert was given on April 16, 1850, with the celebrated European pianist Henri Herz as the star attraction. There was certainly music in the Stockton Minstrels' shows in the Eagle the previous September. And Signor V. Bona, "of the New York Theaters," leading a small orchestra in the overture to Auber's *The Bronze Horse* in the same playhouse on October 18 when it opened with *The Bandit Chief*, established another musical milestone. But the first real concert belonged to Herz. It took place in the New Hall at Front and M streets, with the pianist assisted by Mr. S. Brown, singer; Mrs. Reed, cornet; and Mr. G. Petinos, piano. Tickets sold for $4.

The *Dramatic Chronicle* of San Francisco, several years after the fact, printed an account of the affair which, if accurate, shows something of the difficulties and rewards of making art in the Gold Rush.

Herz had already had considerable success in 14 concerts in San Francisco; one of his rewards was a pan full of gold amounting to 10,000 francs. At 44 he was one of Europe's most brilliant concert stars, if somewhat derided in certain quarters for superficiality and showmanship. He had begun a tour of America and Mexico in 1845 that was to last six years. In collaboration with Stephen Massett—the showman and rolling stone who had been on hand at the opening of the Eagle—he decided to pan for gold among Sacramento audiences, and according to the *Chronicle* designed a concert hall, which was built within a fortnight. Here is the *Chronicle's* account of the first program:

At the hour announced for the concert, the tickets were sold, the house was crowded, the artist was at his post, and everything in readiness except the piano. In consequence of the inexplicable delay, the instrument had not yet arrived. Herz looked at his rough and bearded auditory in a very agreeable trepidation. What if the gold dig-

The celebrated Henri Herz performed at the piano in the city's first formal concert.

One of the true characters of Sacramento and the West was Stephen C. Massett, singer, composer, author, auctioneer and drifter.

Artist George H. Baker did this Independent City Guards Quick Step sheet music.

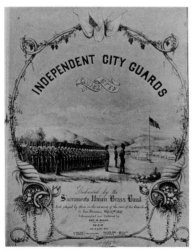

ging dilettanti should take it into their heads to give him a taste of revolver or bowie knife, by the way of filling up the time? Heavy drops of perspiration stood on the frightened pianist's brow, and he began to wish himself in China, or anywhere but California. The miners saw his alarm and kindly comforted him. "Never mind the cussed piano," said two or three of them soothingly, "we don't care for it; we came to see you. Make us a speech."

Herz, restored to serenity, did the best he could. The spoken entertainment seemed to please the audience; and everybody, except the artist, had quite forgotten all about the piano, when its arrival was announced. A number of strong men carried the instrument into the hall and placed it on the platform. It was a three cornered, or "grand" piano, and Herz, promising himself to astonish these simple and easily satisfied inhabitants of the Pacific Coast, seated himself on an empty whisky keg (instead of the more civilized stool) and ran his fingers over the keyboard. Blum! Blum! splash! splash! not a sound did the piano utter, save that of the keys striking the water. The Californians, who had brought the box from San Francisco, finding it very heavy, had floated it into town, and upon dragging it out from the levee, had neglected to pour the water from the interior.

Massett shared the spotlight with Herz in two subsequent concerts, on April 18 and 20, with the price of tickets pushed up to $7. After that the city was never without music for very long. Signor Bona gave "a grand musical concert assisted by 15 musicians of acknowledged talent" as a benefit for himself at the Tehama Theater. As noted, Fanny Manten and a company from Milan offered a ballet, *Gasperone*, at the Pacific on May 20, in a show which also included a magician and ventriloquist. There were orchestras of some sort in all the play-houses and musical entertainment in the saloons. Broadsides of popular ballads were sold in the streets, and by 1853, Atwill and Company had opened the first music store, at 155 J Street. The following year, on November 15, 1854, the German and Swiss immigrants, in keeping with a long European tradition, formed a singing society called the Turner Harmonie, a male chorus which rehearsed in the new Turner Hall. The chorus gave its first concert the following June to celebrate the first birthday of the Turn Verein, in the Tivoli House on the American River, and is still giving concerts in 1973.

In 1855 John McNeill, a 27-year-old New Englander who had come west three years before, organized a male singing organization called the Philharmonic Society. In 14 years the group gave 45 concerts. A singing club of one kind or another was to bear the McNeill name for nearly 100 years.

Band concerts, too, were an integral part of the city's life. A march called "Independent City Guards," published in 1858, declares on its cover that the Sacramento Union Brass Band organized a year before by August Wetterman, was "undoubtedly the finest in the state." George Baker, pioneer Sacramento artist and engraver, published the score; Dale and Company (formerly Atwill) sold it. Richard Dale was also in the business of publishing music, including such long-lasting ballads as "Put Me in My Little Bed" and "Birdie's Lament" by San Francisco composer George T. Evans.

Everybody sang. Songs were published and performed in the service of commerce, temperance, and politics. The influential musician Hugo L. Yanke, also known as Hugo Mansfeldt, wrote and published "Bugbey's Champagne

Galop" to honor the wine business of Benjamin N. Bugbey of Folsom; Bugbey's bearded face adorns the cover, along with an explosively effervescent bottle of champagne. In May, 1859, some Sacramentans formed a local branch of the Dashaway Club, devoted to the downfall of John Barleycorn. Membership grew rapidly—to 459 by January—and the happy abstainers were soon joining in their own "Song of the Dashaways (Dedicated to the Brotherhood)":

> O! all ye friends of Temp'rance
> Come listen to my lay,
> I've ceased to be a tippler,
> I am a Dashaway!

Chorus: Dash! dash the cup away!
Dash! dash the cup away!
In brotherhood, 't is understood,
We'll dash, dash the cup away!

As for music in politics, General Ulysses S. Grant and his managers were alert to the uses of music in his campaign for the presidency in 1868, organizing the Grant Glee Club in Sacramento. The club, in turn, published the *Pacific Grant Songster*, including "The News from Vermont," "written . . . on receipt of the election news from Vermont and sung . . . at the great Mass Meeting held at Sacramento September 4, 1868, creating the wildest enthusiasm." The book included such other stirring numbers as "Come, Honest Voters, One and All, Let Every Republican Rally Around"; "Stand Up for Grant and Colfax"; "Let Traitors Rule No More"; and "Viva L'America."

In such a musical atmosphere, it was no wonder that touring artists did well in the concert halls. The first famous one to follow Herz was Boston-born Elisa Biscaccianti, who was called America's first prima donna. Already a sen-

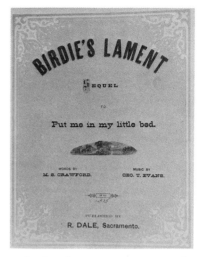

Richard Dale put Sacramento in the music publishing scene with such offerings as this one by Crawford and Evans.

Dale and Company's music store stood on J Street and was active in the sale of instruments and sheet music, with occasional whirls at music publishing.

The first musical organization of record in the city was the Turner Harmonie, founded in 1854 and still singing. This portrait was taken in 1870.

sation in Europe, she came west in February, 1852, and captivated the pioneers. In a year, before taking off for new triumphs in South America, she gave no less than 35 concerts in San Francisco, 13 in Sacramento, seven in Stockton, four in Sonora, three in Marysville, three in Columbia, three in Downieville, one at Park's Bar, and one at Shaw's Flat.

Catherine Hayes, the Swan of Erin, followed her a year later. In 1854, two more celebrated European stars were in Sacramento. The opera singer Madame Anna Bishop was thought to be the real-life original of the heroine in *Trilby*. Her programs ranged from the Mad Scene from *Lucia di Lammermoor* to *The Irish Immigrant's Lament*. The second was the great, eccentric Norwegian violinist, Ole Bornemann Bull. In August, 1854, with the celebrated pianist Maurice Strakosch, he gave a concert which included a set of Paganini variations, one of his own compositions called "The Mother's Prayer," "The Carnival of Venice," and "The Soldier's Dream." They were the vanguard of a parade of great music makers that is still going on.

*Painting
Comes of Age*

"Come, Baker," said B.T. Martin, Esq., lately of Chelsea, Massachusetts, "row off into the stream and make a sketch of the city." George Holbrook Baker, also from Massachusetts and a man who could not be near a pencil without using it to draw, complied. The year was 1849. The sketch Baker made shows five sailing vessels, sails furled, anchored in a wide expanse of water. Two were from Spain, three from New England, including one that belonged to Martin. Behind them, dwarfed by an irregular line of huge trees along the east bank of the Sacramento River, lie the buildings of the infant city of Sacramento, among them Sam Brannan's big store. Thirty-six years later, another Massachusetts artist, George A. Frost, was commissioned to make a painting from the sketch. It now hangs in the California State Library.

Almost from the first days, artists were on hand to record the Gold Rush. Some of them came to dig or pan for gold; all of those we remember eventually took up pencil, pen, or brush, or went to the printer's stone, to give us fascinating views of the place, the time, and the people.

Baker was one of the first. At 22, he quit his art studies in New York and literally fought his way across Mexico to reach California and the gold fields. Once here, he soon lost the fever and went into one business after another. In 1852, he settled down for 10 years in Sacramento. There was plenty for an artist to do, and he also became part of the engraving firm of Barber and Baker, which in 1855 brought out a historic volume called *Sacramento Illustrated*, full of Baker drawings. It sold for $1 a copy then. The price now would be about $750 or more.

Baker drawings appeared on letterheads; were sold in the streets as engravings for a few cents to the pioneers, who sent them back east to their friends and relations; and found such other uses as recording the premium winners at the horse races at the state fair. The pictures graced the publications of the State Agricultural Society when it began to publish its proceedings in 1858.

Up in the hills, George V. Cooper, who had arrived in Sacramento July 19, 1849, along with a storekeeper named John M. Letts, was drawing scenes from the life of the miners, including one showing an artist doing so. Like all the other artists, Cooper also drew Sacramento City and the river and the bustling Embarcadero, including the famous view from the foot of J Street. By 1852, Letts, now back in New York, had enough of them to publish *California Illustrated*, 244 pages of text and Cooper pictures, for a public avid for a look at the Gold Rush.

Another wandering artist who came to stay was Edwin Allen Sherman, a veteran of the Mexican War, who reached town on July 2, 1849, and walked out to Sutter's Fort—Sutter called it New Helvetia—to paint it in the evening, the light filtering out of its main gate, with Sam Brannan's early store nearby in the twilight.

It was an age which bought engravings to thrill to the latest sensational events. Pictures like the *View of the Fire in Sacramento City*, depicting a holocaust on the Embarcadero November 2 and 3, 1852, were a prime source of an artist's livelihood. But some, like William S. Jewett, did quite well with portraiture. Jewett left a promising career in his native New York to join the rush to California in 1849. His extant portraits include an oval oil of General John A. Sutter, in full uniform complete with epaulets, painted in 1856 in San Francisco, and a large family portrait of Andrew Jackson Grayson, his wife and young son, depicted as they might have paused in the Sierra to gaze toward the goal of their arduous journey west in 1846. Grayson, later to be known as the Audubon of the Pacific for his own talent and passion for art and ornithology, commissioned Jewett's work in 1850 for $2,000. Its fate is typical of much nineteenth century art. First famous enough to be exhibited in many parts of the state, it dropped out of sight for decades, to be rediscovered in 1941 in the dark hallway of a farmhouse near St. Helena, Napa County.

Another eastern artist who arrived in 1849 was T. A. Ayres. Like others, he tried his luck at finding gold, at Tuttletown, but soon returned to the more

Ole Bull, known around the world for his violin mastery, first appeared in Sacramento in August, 1854.

productive passion of painting. His place in California history was assured
when, in 1855, he went along with the James M. Hutchings party to make what
was the first "tourist" trip through Yosemite Valley. The effective discovery
by Europeans had taken place only four years before. The publication of his
sketches, including one of "The Yo-semite Falls," drew national attention to
the great valley. Ayres went back to make more drawings, then put all the
views into a celebrated painted panorama (a popular form of entertainment in
the late nineteenth century) which enjoyed a successful run in McNulty's Hall
in Sacramento. But Ayres did not live long to capitalize on this success; he went
down with the schooner *Laura Bevan*, bound for Santa Barbara from San Pedro, in 1858.

Lerck's Office of the District Court of the Northern dist.^t of California.

Lith. Britton & Rey S.Francisco

TO JAMESTOWN
CAL.

George Henry Goddard came to Sacramento in 1850 and did many scenes for the lithographers of the day, including this *Southern Approach to Jamestown*. He later gained prominence as a geologist and was honored by having the second highest peak in the Sierra named after him.

Paintings or drawings, panoramas or prints, the art of those first two decades in Sacramento and its environs constitutes a precious record of remarkable variety. We know how the scattered buildings of the early mining towns looked against the low rolling hills and oaks and evergreens, thanks to lithographs like *Southern Approach to Jamestown, Tuolumne County*, by George Henry Goddard, and the view of Coloma in the *California Views* of the early engraving firm of Kuchel and Dresel. (Goddard, already a surveyor, architect, and painter when he arrived in Sacramento in 1850, eventually gained a lasting fame in geology, geography, and mineraology as well. Mount Goddard, second highest peak in the Sierra, is named for him. Charles C. Kuchel was the great uncle of former California Senator Thomas H. Kuchel.)

Carl Wilhelm Hahn, a prize-winning painter in his native Saxony before he came to California in 1867, left us such scenes as *Sacramento Railroad Station* (1874, De Young Museum, San Francisco), *Harvest Time, Sacramento Valley* (1875, Palace of the Legion of Honor, San Francisco), and *San Francisco Market* (Crocker Gallery, Sacramento). Andrew P. Hill recorded the look of the Yolo County farm of John Wolfskill in 1873, with its profusion of livestock and its neat, handsome buildings. Gideon J. Denny, who arrived in 1849, made a specialty of marine subjects, like the steamship *Senator*, perhaps the most famous and best loved of all the old river steamers. Stephen William Shaw, another '49er, became the most successful portrait painter in California. (Among examples of his work in the Crocker Gallery are portraits of Judge E.B.Crocker himself and of Thomas Hill, painter of the celebrated *The Driving of the Last Spike*.)

The artists in Sacramento were especially drawn to the Sacramento River as a subject. Artists Baker and Cooper left us the very earliest views; a few years later, George Tirrell's painting of the waterfront as seen from the Yolo County side shows a remarkably busier array of shipping, including sidewheelers of all sizes. (Tirrell's *Panorama of California*, 25,300 square feet of canvas which premiered in San Francisco in 1860, was said to be the longest panorama of them all.) James Lamson painted the Yolo-Sacramento swing bridge, the first swing span in California, completed in 1858 at a cost of $60,000. (*Bridge at Sacramento* now hangs in the museum of the California Historical Society in San Francisco.) And Norton Bush, who came to California at 29 from his native New York in 1853, was among those who saw the river as a place of beauty as well as commerce, industry, and history. Witness his oil of the sternwheeler *Governor Dana*, seen against the majestic trees along the bank—presumably upstream from Sacramento, since the *Dana* traveled between the capital and the Feather River district.

Artist T. A. Ayres did the sketch at right of Tuttletown in 1855. He was the first artist to sketch the wonders of Yosemite, next page, when he traveled there with James M. Hutchings. They brought nationwide attention to Yosemite with their words and drawings.

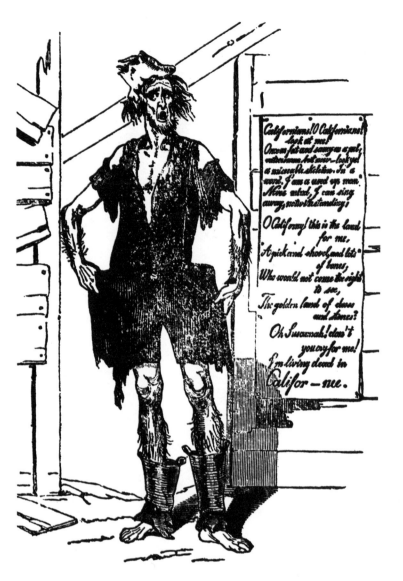

Charles Christian Nahl was one of California's best known artists. He arrived in 1850 and tried his luck as miner at Rough and Ready and eventually set up shop in Sacramento; much of his early work went up in the 1852 fire. He worked in many media, and while some critics thought his art overly dramatic, he left a rich legacy of his times. These woodcuts are The Used-Up Man (*top left*), A Well Known Banking House (*bottom left*), A Live Woman at the Mines (*top right*), and The Miner's Sunday (*bottom right*).

William S. Jewett was a successful painter in New York before he moved to the West in 1849. He had a studio on Front Street and painted some of the leading families of the day, such as this one of the Andrew Jackson Graysons and their child.

Perhaps the most famous of all Gold Rush paintings is Charles Christian Nahl's *Sunday Morning in the Mines*, 1872, which hangs in the E. B. Crocker Art Gallery. Full of the vivid detail beloved of genre painters, it contrasts such hectic activities as drinking and horse racing, in one half of the canvas, with the sobriety of reading and washing clothes in the other.

Nahl knew his subject at first hand. A member of a German family whose artistic history went back three centuries, he arrived in California with his mother and brother in 1850, at the age of 32, and for a time tried his luck at mining at Rough and Ready. After a stay in Marysville, he set up shop in Sacramento as an artist. The fire of 1852 destroyed much of his work and he moved to San Francisco. He maintained ties with the capital, however, obtaining from among others the patronage of Judge E. B. Crocker. In 1858 he and his brother and partner, Arthur, won prizes in the state fair art exhibit.

Popular and successful from the outset of his career, Nahl nevertheless was sometimes criticized in the press for his "overwrought" color and the theatrical attitudes of his figures. To modern eyes, these things seem no more than typical of a great deal of the painting of his age, in Europe as well as America. Eugen Neuhaus, a modern California art authority who has studied him, calls attention to his notable draftsmanship, his "courageous and positive use of color" and the fact that his pictures of California life remain "convincing, expressive, vital records of a vital age."

Less well known than *Sunday Morning in the Mines* is Nahl's *Murieta* (Press and Union League Club, San Francisco), a strikingly romantic view of the colorful bandit of the early 1850s, eyes glaring, hair flying, a knife in his upraised hand, astride a black horse galloping up a rocky mountain pass. Another is *Indian Boy with Dogs* (DeYoung Museum, San Francisco), a meticulously painted, superbly composed study of a young chief of the Yuba Indians. The very grown-up "boy" was Wahla, a member of northern California's Maidu

Tribe. He was educated by Milton S. Latham, who was governor of California for five days in 1860, resigning to serve as U.S. Senator. Wahla is seen seated on a grassy bank in rather formal dress—a dark coat and trousers, white shirt, dark bow tie, his strong features serious but pleasant. One handsome spotted hunting dog lies at his left, another stands at his right. In the foreground, chickens wander; in the background, the hills of the valley recede into the haze.

Of all the artists who painted the beauties of the country around early Sacramento, history so far has awarded the most honor and credited the most influence to William Keith and Albert Bierstadt.

Both were European born, brought to America as children. Keith, who has been called an "old master of California," was a native of Aberdeenshire, Scotland, who arrived in California in 1859 at the age of 21 on a roving commission from Harper & Brothers, for whom he had been a wood engraver. Returning to Scotland after a short time, by 1862 he was back in the San Francisco Bay area, which was to remain his home until his death. A friend of John Muir, he was drawn to the California landscape, traveling often in the Sierra and the Sacramento Valley, sketching and painting. William F. Jackson, later the longtime director of the E. B. Crocker Art Gallery, was a Keith student and sometimes accompanied him on these tours. The gallery has a sizeable Keith collection. The great San Francisco fire of 1906 destroyed some 2,000 of his drawings and paintings. He survived them by five years.

This curious painting is Nahl's *Indian Boy with Dogs*.

Bierstadt, to become even more a world-wide celebrity in his lifetime, was born in Germany in 1830. Brought to America at the age of two, by the time he was 20 he was already advertising himself as a teacher of painting in New Bedford, Massachusetts. In 1863, now well known, he made his first trip to California; from 1871 to 1873, a member of both the National Academy of the United States and the Legion of Honor of France, he returned to tour the bay region, the Sacramento Valley and the Sierra extensively; in 1884, he made sill another such trip. His views, often monumental in scope, were enormously influential and carried the sights of California all over the world. The German royal family, for instance, acquired a Bierstadt painting of California redwoods.

No account of art in the early decades of Sacramento would be complete without a note of the presence of two persons who were not themselves artists, but who were to exercise a major role in the future cultural life of the city: Judge and Mrs. E. B. Crocker.

Edwin Bryant Crocker, older brother of the Charles Crocker who became one of the Big Four which built the Central Pacific Railroad, left a law practice in Indiana to migrate to California in 1852. He was 34. He and his bride, the former Margaret Rhodes, had been married only a short time before the journey.

The Crockers prospered in Sacramento, and both soon became active in civic, cultural, and charitable affairs. The impulses that led eventually to the E. B. Crocker Art Gallery can be found in the earlier lives of both. In Indiana, Crocker had been an ardent abolitionist, defending fugitive slaves at his own expense. In Sacramento, this strain of idealism found an outlet not only in the administration of justice—when Governor Stanford named him to the State Supreme Court—but in civic life. He found time, for instance, to help form the

Sacramento Musical Society and to serve as its first president. Margaret Crocker, meanwhile, became known for her unostentatious charities. Both gave generously to churches, asylums, and schools.

In 1870 the Crockers made an extensive tour of Europe. Personally and through dealers they bought a large collection of art and shipped it home. The works included old masters and presumed old masters, much painting of the time by European artists and, almost incidentally, a large number of drawings. The drawings, more than 60 years later, were to be evaluated as one of the world's notable collections, including first rate examples of the work of such artists as Albrecht Dürer, Peter Paul Rubens, William Hogarth, Rembrandt Van Rijn, Jacob Jordaens and others.

In 1871, construction began on a gallery on the southeast corner of 2nd and

O streets—directly behind the large Crocker home, which stood on the south-west corner of 3rd and O facing 3rd Street. The gallery, full of beautiful materials and meticulous workmanship, was completed at a cost of $200,000.

In 1875 Judge Crocker died. According to the testimony of his contemporaries, he had always wished that the Crocker art collection should be used to enrich the life of the city. His widow made the gallery increasingly available to the public, and in 1885 deeded the gallery and its collection to the City of Sacramento, to be administered in joint tenancy with the California Museum Association, which had been formed the year before under the leadership of David Lubin. The gallery, which claims to be the oldest museum in the west, still operates under that management. It has been not only a focal point for visual art but one of the city's important concert halls since its very first years.

Charles C. Kuchel and Emil Dresel were one of the most important artistic teams in early California lithography. Their series of California Views included Nevada City and other major cities and mining towns.

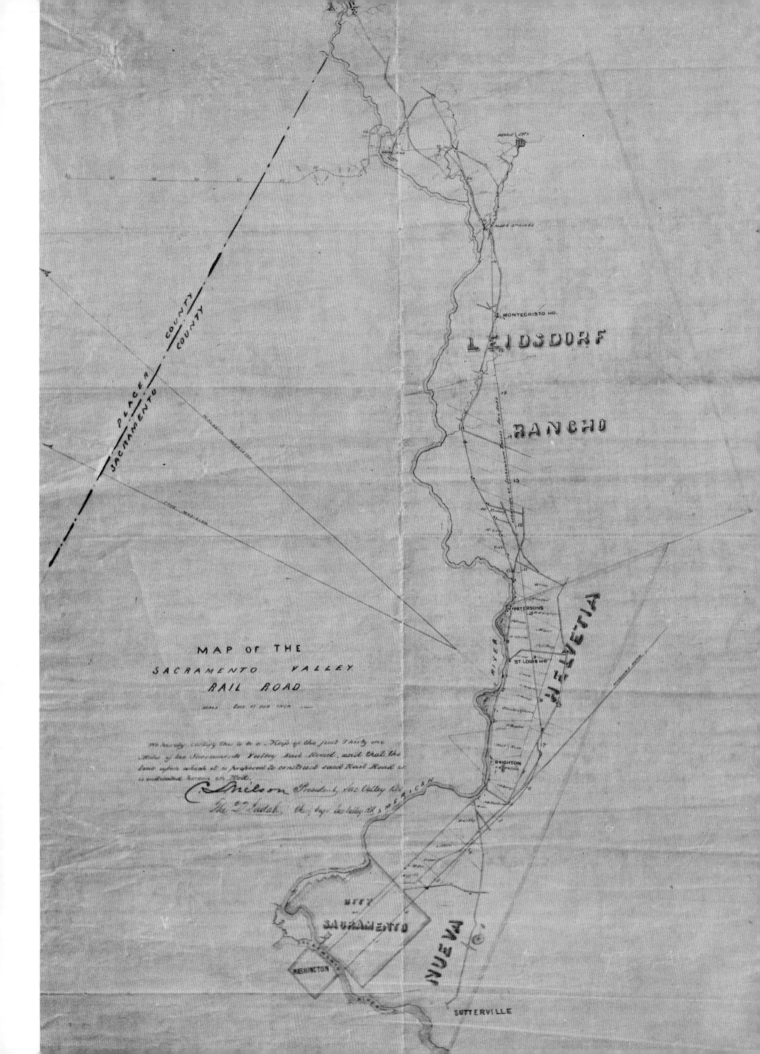

MAP OF THE

SACRAMENTO VALLEY

RAIL ROAD

Transportation and Communication

Chapter Eight

No OUTPOST, NO CIVILIZATION is sufficient unto itself, totally self-reliant. It is connected to the whole by the tenuous strings of communication and transportation and trade. Without that pipeline, that lifeline, growth is smothered and the creation becomes a poor and withered thing, entrapped, and eventually it dies.

So it was with Sacramento City, the boomtown which exploded on the banks of the Sacramento River outside the walls of Sutter's Fort, with the discovery of gold in the Sierra nearby. From the beginning it was a city fed and fleshed by transportation: by wagon team, by freighter, by riverboat, and finally by iron rails laid by iron men across the great mountain ranges to the east.

It was Captain Sutter who first brought European civilization to the inland valleys. And he came by boat, a captain-admiral of a small expedition of three vessels, one little more than a small scow. His "fleet" was to be the forerunner of a time when the Sacramento literally was to become a forest of masts and when great river steamers fought to establish new records on the San Francisco-to-Sacramento run, their holds burdened with freight.

In the first blush of the gold trade, profits on freighting were running 200 to 300 per cent, with shipping approaching fifty dollars a ton. One account reads:

"A number of small vessels were plying the river, and small schooners from thirty to one hundred and fifty tons readily brought from five to twenty thousand dollars, while the finest merchant vessels were lying in the [San Francisco] bay and could hardly be sold for sufficient to pay port dues." The passage on these vessels was from $25 to $50; with the privilege of finding and cooking your own provisions on the way. The passage generally occupied from four to six days, and a sad experience of the "musquito (sic) kingdom."

The bark *Whiton*, which was to become Sacramento's first post office, arrived early in 1849, with the first cargo of merchandise dispatched to the new city from the Atlantic coast. The *Eliodora*, which arrived in March, two months

The old embarcadero where Sacramento was born became the prime supply point for railroad construction, holding tons of iron and steel destined for the mountains.

Judah proposed the railroad line at left in 1854. His practical approach and engineering skill were to spell success where others failed.

The California Stage Company became the most extensive of its day when it consolidated several lines in 1853 and crushed all opposition for a few years.

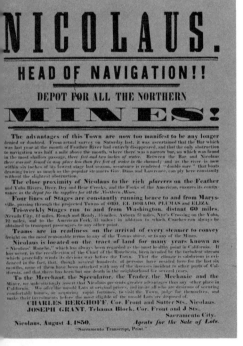

previously, is said to have been the first square-rigged vessel to ascend the river. The first steam craft to ply the Sacramento waters, the *Sitka*, reportedly was outfitted at San Francisco and dispatched to Sutter's Fort. Newspaper accounts suggest the small steam craft went up the Sacramento in November 1847 and made the return passage in six days. On the return it was beaten to Benicia by four days by an ox team which left the Embarcadero at the same time.

In July, 1849, the steamboat *Sacramento* was put under construction—the first to be built in the city exclusively for Sacramento-San Francisco trading—about a mile above the city, and was launched three months later. The Edward Everett Company launched a small steamer for Sacramento trading in August, but it shortly was lost in waters upstream from Sacramento. The Yuba Company also built a small scow steamer with the intention of using it for dredging, but freight was bringing such a premium it was pressed into service to Yuba City and Marysville. On one passage it carried bricks for one dollar a brick and lumber at $150 per thousand board feet. The small steamer *Mint* arrived in October and later the same month, the steamer *McKim* tied up at the Embarcadero to the boom of welcoming cannon—boasting 60 berths and 200 horsepower. Its rates for the San Francisco run: cabin, $30; deck, $20; freight, $50 a ton; berths, $5; meals, $1.50. The *McKim* made a $16,000 profit on one passage alone.

Of course such success, such demand, became father to a rash of construction of new river vessels, and the pursuit of passage records. The steamer *Senator* made the passage in 22 hours in November, 1848, upstream, and in nine hours on the return passage; thus it became the first to negotiate the round trip in one day. *Sacramento Illustrated*, in a play on words, mused: "Every new *Enterprise* is *Eclipsed* by some new one, and is but the forerunner of some new *Surprise*." All were in passage on the Sacramento River.

With such competition came tragedy. The riverboat, with its boilers, was a floating bomb; several blew. On January 27, 1854, for example, the steamer *Pearl* blew while on a return trip from Marysville. For several days the river was dragged. Seventy bodies were recovered and many persons were wounded. Corpses were laid out in the Water Works building for public view so identification might be established. The sight moved the *Sacramento Illustrated* to lament: "Many a form lay there, unknown and unwept, in the habiliments of death, that in another land, far away was the object of a parent's love and care, and had many a warm friend whose heart vibrated with emotion, as this fearful tale of death was told. Very few of those who thus perished by this terrible casualty were claimed or recognized. . . . All business of the city suspended. Over three thousand people attended the funeral."

Yes, there were, in the early years of river navigation, dozens of shipwrecks, explosions, mishaps—but the river was a lifeline to the bay ports, and the beltline for transportation to the gold fields. At the height of the search for color, the Embarcadero became a graveyard for ships; for few captains could keep crews to man the ships, so strong was the lure of gold. To give a quick glimpse of the kind of traffic which burdened the Sacramento in the gold years, consider this: in the year 1851, height of the gold fever, records listed eight barks, 23 brigs, 195 schooners, five sloops, 173 steamers and 24 barges. How

By 1860 a regular stage line had been established as far north as Portland, Oregon. This rather romanticized lithograph shows one of the stages in northern California.

many passengers they brought is unknown, but they brought some 250,000 tons of goods—small compared to the shipping to Sacramento only two years later: 415,000 tons.

Sacramento's very location, situated as it is at the confluence of two great rivers and centrally located in the great valley, made it inevitable it would become a transportation center, when the horde of miners inundated Sacramento.

James Birch, who originally was a seeker of gold, then became the first to found a major stage and freight line, launched his new venture in 1849. The line went from Sacramento to Mormon Island. Passengers paid a minimum of $16 for the 20-mile ride, and as much as $32, depending upon the condition of the roads and the number of people waiting for service.

Birch probably was the first to appreciate just how big a profit there was in stage and freight enterprises. He proceeded to establish a transportation network feeding into all of the mining settlements, and his profits were immense. He organized the first stage company in California, the California Stage Company, with a capital stock of $700,000, in 1853, and established offices in the Orleans Hotel on 2nd between J and K. By 1856 the company had 80 coaches, 125 wagons, and 1,100 horses plying 24 main routes. By the outbreak of the

Civil War, he had extended his operations to as far distant a point as Portland, Oregon.

There is this account, paraphrased, of the Sacramento scene at the height of the population and business explosion in the gold years:

By count, at one time there were 217 wagons and carts lined up along the levee, loading and departing with full loads. Sidewalks were "covered, crowded, heaped with bales, boxes, packages, bags, barrels and bundles." Mule teams filled the streets as did men "evidently from the mountains, strong built, hairy-faced, dark complected in woolen shirts, coarse pantaloons and miner boots. . . ."

The Adams Express Company was located on 2nd Street in 1852 when this picture was taken. The company was the first to link the mines to the Atlantic seaboard but it failed in the panic of 1855 after spirited competition with Wells Fargo.

The river was a highway from the sea, and from the first whispers of gold it became a crowded thoroughfare. This view from the *Placer Times and Transcript* shows the *Senator* in the foreground with plenty of company.

The city was using about 10 per cent of the tonnage being shipped to the Embarcadero, reshipping 15 per cent to up-river stations and dispatching the remaining 75 per cent to the mining area with six- and eight-mule teams. Some 300 to 400 tons of goods a day were being teamed out at the height of the shipping. One early day Sacramentan, accounts suggest, counted 1,464 wagons on the road from Sacramento to the mines in El Dorado County; so thick was the traffic that the old Willow Springs Hotel, 25 miles from Sacramento en route to Coloma, was serving some 130 people daily, and was preparing lunches for 350 more.

The trek to the Gold Country took a special kind of wagon, moreover. The old Conestoga, of comparative gentle framing, could hardly survive the Sierra trails. So freighters produced the California Wagon—weighing some two tons, dry weight, and capable of holding another six tons of freight. And mules were the preferred beast of burden.

But mules were not the only animals introduced to the freight runs. In the late 1850s, the traveler might think he was being exposed to a mirage, Sahara-style. For around the twisting trail might emerge a camel caravan, according to some reports. Spurred by the cries of rugged mule drivers, the baggage-laden animals ambled uneasily.

When the federal government dispatched camels to the deserts of the Southwest as a shipping experiment, California and Nevada traders saw in the experiment a potential new source of freight power. Several enterprising merchants, plagued with increasing demand for shipping of salt to the mines of Washoe County in Nevada, acquired several camels on an experimental basis, to augment the recalcitrant mule trains. The experiment failed.

There were still other experiments in transportation, however. In the 1860s, for example, an enterprising trader in Quincy, in Plumas County, hitched a couple of crossbreeds of Newfoundlands and St. Bernards to a sled and set up a profitable snow express service to isolated, snowbound settlements

in the mountains. The sled could handle 250 pounds of precious freight, and one passenger. It may not have made its owner, a J. B. Whiting, wealthy, but it did win him a place in Gold Country history.

It was 1855. Sacramento had a population of approximately 15,000. The city had a trade approaching six million dollars a month and was doing about three million dollars of business each month in gold trade. And there were dreamers, like Colonel Charles Lincoln Wilson, who thought in terms of a new empire: railroading. His dream led to the establishment of California's first railroad: the Sacramento Valley Rail Road. And this venture, in turn, was to become the first leg of what would, in the next 14 years, lead to the final spanning of the nation from seaboard to seaboard.

The birth of the old S.V.R.R., from its railhead in Sacramento to its terminus in Folsom, 22 miles distant, was not easy. It was spanked into life in the midst of a great money panic. Materials and equipment had to be shipped around the Horn. Its cry of life was to be strangled more than once by pains of birth but finally—some seven months and $1,380,000 after the first rail was laid on August 9, 1855—the railroad was completed to Folsom.

This new road, first to be chartered west of the Rockies as well as in California, was incorporated August 16, 1852, by Wilson, who had journeyed to California as a gold seeker from his native Maine at the height of the 1849 Gold Rush. He had, by 1852, been gold miner, operator of a steamer on the Sacramento, then contractor for the construction of a plank road over San Francisco's sand dunes. He was the S.V.R.R.'s first president. He had as his vice president a young man named William Tecumseh Sherman, who later was to earn fame as a Civil War general, and who helped to lay out Sacramento in 1848.

Preparing for the road, Wilson went back to the East in 1854 in search of an engineer. He approached a young man named Theodore Dehone Judah. Would Judah be interested in acting as engineer for Wilson's proposed new road? Judah would. He wired his wife at their Niagara Falls home: "We sail for California April 2." It was the culmination of a dream for Judah, who long had envisioned the construction of the first transcontinental railroad. Arriving in

The *L. L. Robinson* of the Sacramento Valley Line, stands for a portrait. Some say Judah's face is seen beneath the top hat.

Sacramento in late May, the first question that had to be resolved was routing. Should the roadbed be routed east in a projection of M Street, cutting through most of the farms, or along the natural lines of R Street? Judah recommended R Street and raised the hope the construction might, by chance, turn up a new Mother Lode of gold, for the country he said was "impregnated with it."

With grading well underway, a dry winter touched off a money panic. Many of the road's backers forfeited their stock through nonpayment of assessments. Colonel Wilson was the hardest hit. He lost all he owned in a bank failure; even before the first rail was laid, he resigned as president but remained on as a director of the line. Wilson was succeeded by Captain J. L. Folsom, for whom the town of Folsom was named. But in July, 1855, Folsom died, and he, in turn, was succeeded by C. K. Garrison, a San Francisco steamship executive and an early mayor of the Bay City. Financing was increasingly difficult to obtain and so the line was planned to Folsom only, not beyond. On February 20, 1856, the first train pulled into Folsom. A state senator was quoted as referring to the old mule pack train, and as saying: "Today, how different. The iron horse, that mightiest triumph of the human art, pants along the metallic way, tireless and uncurbed in his strength, and impatient to dare the far off." Thus was the way paved for what would follow.

Theodore Judah had the vision and skill to propose spanning the nation by rail.

The S.V.R.R. was but a prologue—grand dream that it was in the year 1855—for the greater adventure, that of bridging the razor-backed Sierra, with its reaching summits and its stunning scene of heaving mountains.

Judah had a greater dream than merely building a line across the valley flats: he was consumed with the ambition of laying steel across the mountains. It was not the dream of an empire builder, as such; it was the dream of an engineer facing the difficult, if not the impossible.

Congress had been considering proposals for a transcontinental line for some time. U.S. Senator Benton of Missouri had proposed, as early as 1849, federal authorization and subsidization of such lines. It was not until 1853 that a survey was undertaken, though. Three potential routes were chosen to find the information necessary for intelligent planning. The more information gathered, the more difficult the passage seemed.

After laying the line for the S.V.R.R. Judah visited Washington personally in 1856 and 1857 to stimulate interest in a transcontinental line; he distributed to Congress a pamphlet called "A Practical Plan For Building The Pacific Railroad." Even then, however, the nation was approaching a crisis over the question of slavery and Union, so much of the argument fell on unresponsive ears.

Of course California needed the Pacific line. In 1859, the state legislature called a Pacific Railroad Convention in San Francisco. The convention produced a formal request to Congress that it assist in the project by granting lands to the state, guaranteeing interest on bonds, and otherwise encouraging, through subsidy, the construction of a line. Delegates to that convention inclined toward a route which would have crossed the Sierra through Stockton, eastward over the Sierra by whatever route the legislature would select. Per-

Rails across the Sierra

Collis P. Huntington

Mark Hopkins

haps the most significant action, however, was the naming of Judah as an accredited California agent in the nation's capital. Congressman J. C. Burch of Weaverville agreed to sponsor legislation that same year, but the nation was even nearer to war in 1859, and so the measure was put over to 1860.

While in the East, Judah used his persuasive skills, and his engineering determination, to complete studies of locomotives. He found that capacity of locomotives, developed to that time, would allow slopes of 350 feet per mile. This gave hope, encouraged investment; up to this determination, most believed the locomotive, as engineered to that time, would be incapable of negotiating grades necessary to Sierra construction.

Judah met disappointment after disappointment. He felt that the organization of a private company might stir Congress to action; he was beginning to lose faith in the government support of a road. So with a good friend, Dr. Daniel Strong of Dutch Flat, he proposed a route through Dutch Flat as a bridge point for the Sierra. They wrote articles for incorporation and stock subscription papers, and they gave a name to the proposal: the Central Pacific Railroad.

The first effect of this action was recrimination. The S.V.R.R., sensing competition, removed Judah as S.V.R.R. chief engineer. Undisturbed, Judah published a report in November, 1860, promoting the Dutch Flat route as the best approach through the Sierra.

Meanwhile, Strong had gathered subscriptions of more than $46,000 from the communities of Dutch Flat, Illinois Town (Colfax), Grass Valley, and Nevada City; but another $70,000 was needed to comply with the laws of California. It would be necessary, Judah and Strong decided, to approach businessmen in San Francisco—and perhaps Sacramento—for support. San Francisco gave the idea the coolest of receptions, however. San Franciscans feared that a route giving Sacramento the terminus would endanger business in San Francisco. Spurned by San Francisco, Judah and Strong organized a meeting of some 30 Sacramento businessmen to be held in the St. Charles Hotel on J between 8th and 9th. In that group were four men destined to go down in history as the Big Four, men of varied wealth, backgrounds, inclinations, tempers, but men who would work together:

Collis P. Huntington, 39, who arrived in Sacramento from New York in 1849 after financing his trip, with a little left over for investment, by conducting a baggage transport operation across the Isthmus of Panama while awaiting passage to San Francisco. He was married with a family when he left the East. Frugal, energetic, a no-nonsense man, he went into the hardware business in Sacramento with

Mark Hopkins, another New Yorker, who settled in Sacramento after a brief business venture in Placerville. The oldest of the Big Four at 49, he also was the frailest. He, too, was a no-nonsense man inclined toward the private life and unlike

Charles Crocker, who, before his association with the railroad, had served on the Sacramento City Council and in the state legislature. He came west with two brothers, worked in the gold diggings briefly, then in 1852 opened a dry goods store in Sacramento. The next two years he accumulated rather substantial wealth. He was an astute businessman, and was quite young, 38, when he joined the Big Four, as was

Leland Stanford, a New York attorney who came west to join four brothers already in business in Sacramento. He was 36 when he joined the railroad venture and got his start supplying miners at Michigan Bluff before settling in Sacramento in 1855. His grocery and supply ventures were to make him independently wealthy and to give him the time to satisfy his instinctive search for political power—an instinct which would bring to him the distinction of becoming California's first Republican governor and Civil War governor. Of the four, Stanford had the strongest sense of public relations; and he became, more or less, the spokesman for the venture, and its contact with the public.

At the meeting that night in the St. Charles Hotel, Judah explained his plan, spoke persuasively of its potential as an investment and excited both the curiosity and the sense of adventure of the Sacramentans present. He told them a complete survey of the proposed route would be necessary but he expressed conviction that the plan not only was feasible, it was practical.

Collis Huntington eventually persuaded his cautious business partner, Hopkins, along with Crocker, Stanford, Lucius Booth, James Bailey, and Charles Marsh, to join him and Judah in financing the survey.

Then came government complications. The two houses of Congress got around to passing a railroad bill in the session of 1860–61, but the House called for two roads and the Senate three. The imminent clash between the North and the South would ease the complication, however—and the Civil War would prod Congress to move to give both authority and assistance to the proposed construction, for transportation would be urgently necessary to the North.

So on June 28, 1861, the Central Pacific Railroad of California was formally incorporated under a new state law. Stanford was named president, Huntington vice president, Hopkins treasurer and Bailey secretary; Judah was named chief engineer. Crocker was named to the board of directors, without formal office. His genius was in management of men, and in supply, and these became his functions.

Meantime, Judah already was at work on a survey which extended 81 miles from the base of the mountains, reaching an elevation of 7,000 feet. He made skillful use of a natural ridge which limited the maximum rise of the line to 105 feet per mile in this area, well within locomotive capability. By using the Truckee River, he avoided the necessity of scaling a second summit. He was ready to give Congress a reliable report that any predictable problem in pushing a railroad through the Sierra could be resolved.

While Judah was in Washington promoting the project, the Civil War began. And on July 1, 1862, President Abraham Lincoln signed the Pacific Railroad Bill; Southern opposition, now, was no longer a complicating factor. The bill established a five-member commission to administer federal participation. The creation of the Union Pacific Railroad Company to construct the eastern section of a transcontinental line was approved; so was the assignment of the Central Pacific to the western and more difficult portion of the line.

Charles Crocker

Leland Stanford

The Railroad: Finance and Engineering

The frugal Collis Huntington insisted on drawing the plans for the first building constructed by the Central Pacific and then forced its use as the first ticket office.

The bill also set up an intricate arrangement of land grants and financial aid. Federal money was to be distributed at rates ranging from $16,000 to $48,000 per mile, depending on the difficulty of the terrain. A minimum of 50 miles of track had to be laid the first two years, and 50 miles each year thereafter to qualify, except in the mountains where 20 miles per year would be demanded. And the road was to be completed by July 1, 1876.

The provisions were to be amended several times but the train had begun to move. Huntington, in Washington at the time of the passage, wired his colleagues in Sacramento: "We have drawn the elephant, now let us see if we can harness him."

Judah went to work immediately contracting for eight locomotives to be delivered in January along with 5,000 tons of rail, eight passenger cars, four baggage, and 60 freight cars.

Ground was broken at the foot of K Street in Sacramento on January 8th, 1863, and the race was on. That same month, Charles Crocker retired from the board of the C.P.R.R. giving his place to his brother, attorney and later Judge E. B. Crocker.

State Geologist J. D. Whitney was requested by Charles Crocker to make a determination of the base of the Sierra Nevada. The importance of Whitney's services to the construction is clear in the recollection that the company was to receive $48,000 per mile for construction through the mountains, some three times the figure credited to them for flat construction. This made grading and routing vital determinations.

Judah had considered the base of the Sierra to be at Newcastle, 31 miles east of Sacramento, but Whitney ruled the rise actually began at Arcade Creek, just seven miles east. The seeds of controversy over alleged fraud were sown by this and it was not settled until President Lincoln officially accepted Whitney's recommendation the following year.

The mountain base disagreement was just one of many differences which accentuated a break between the Big Four on one hand and Theodore Judah on the other. It has been suggested that by September of 1863, Judah had been offered $100,000 for his shares in the company, with the option to buy out the Big Four if he could raise the capital. Apparently this was his object in leaving for the East full of confidence that the Vanderbilts, or other wealthy interests, would back him in gaining control of the project he considered his. However, he was to die in New York November 2 after contracting yellow fever while crossing Panama.

Joseph L. Folsom

This building was just a store on K Street when its upper floor was used as a meeting place for those who would tackle the Sierra with rails. This is the only known picture of the store.

In the next few months, Judah's friends departed from the company one by one. The Pacific Railroad now was firmly in the hands of those destined to ride it to fortune.

The first locomotive arrived in Sacramento on October 5, 1863, just five days before Judah left for the East. The company had no place to house the engine, named the *Governor Stanford* in honor of the company president. When it arrived, the company had only one little building, built for $150 in a single day. The thrifty Huntington had designed the shed himself rather than pay an architect, and he later was to insist it be used as the first ticket office when the line began carrying passengers.

The Sacramento railroad shops were begun in November, 1861, and they would become an outstanding and productive unit of the railroad. They employed a great number of craftsmen and produced much of the equipment used on the line.

Samuel Skerry Montague was named acting chief engineer after Judah's death. He did not drop the "acting" prefix until 1868; but he did hold the job until he died in 1883. Montague had worked with Judah on the preliminary surveys.

The first paying passengers queued up at Huntington's little shack in April of 1864 to purchase tickets to Junction (Roseville), 18½ miles to the east. Thereafter, trains ran daily to that point while construction continued eastward. In

S. S. Montague succeeded Judah as chief engineer of the Central Pacific.

In this 1866 view of the Central Pacific depot an omnibus awaits travelers to take them to their lodgings. The Water Works is in the background at the foot of I Street.

176

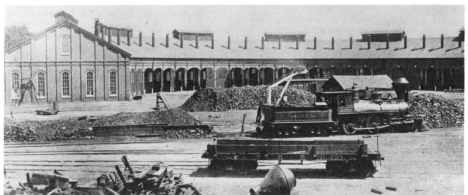

The Russell photograph above shows the impressive machine shops of the Central Pacific. At left is the equally massive roundhouse, a major support facility.

Lisle's Bridge withstood torrential run-offs over the American River until half of it was swept away in the flood of 1862.

June, the line extended to Newcastle. The Dutch Flat and Donner Lake Wagon Road Company opened for business just a few days later, and three days were cut from the journey to Virginia City, where silver was now luring Argonauts.

There were problems other than construction, however. The proprietors of the Sacramento Valley Rail Road, principally L. L. Robinson, had been frustrating the Central Pacific project from the beginning. Now the pesky little

A newspaper artist of the day preserved the trial run of the Sacramento Valley Rail Road's locomotive in 1855.

short line had run track down river to Freeport where the river trade was met. So in 1865 the Central Pacific felt compelled to buy out its competitor for some $800,000. Then it tore up the line to Freeport but maintained the operation to Folsom; it was still turning a profit.

But construction was not moving as rapidly as was necessary to meet requirements for government incentives. Congress cooperated by changing some of the stipulations of the Pacific Railroad Bill but the big problem lay in recruiting a work force big enough to do the job.

Crocker suggested recruiting Chinese from the Auburn area but his partners and the man he had put in charge of construction, J. H. Strobridge, resisted. Five thousand workers were needed; the crews rarely numbered more than 800.

Reluctantly, Strobridge tried 50 Chinese. They impressed him with their industry and strength. He began to hire more, 50 at a time, but the white workers balked at working beside "Celestials." Crocker sternly told them to get back to work or the line would be built with Chinese labor only. Amid scowls and muttered oaths, the men returned to work. As construction demands increased, the Central Pacific began to contract for the importation of Chinese. By 1866, some 10,000 Chinese were in the force working to put steel over the Sierra; and they did the job extremely well.

The activity was all to the east but the business interests of the Big Four boxed the compass. They had absorbed the Sacramento Valley Rail Road in 1865; two years later they cleared the way for an eventual line to San Francisco by purchasing the franchise of the old Western Pacific Railroad. This name-

Sacramento Valley Railroad.

FREIGHT TARIFF.

PAYABLE IN U. S. GOLD COIN OR ITS EQUIVALENT.

DISTANCE	FROM SACRAMENTO TO	CLASS 1 — In Cents, per 100 lbs.	2 — In Cents, per 100 lbs.	3 — In Cents, per 100 lbs.	4 — In Dollars, per car load of 20,000 lbs.	5 — In Dollars, per car load of 20,000 lbs.
	Sacramento					
5	Brighton	4	4	4	5	5
6	Perkins	4	4	4	6	6
7	Freeport Junction	5	5			
10	Mayhew's	7	7	7	10	10
11.5	Routier's	8	8	8	12	11
12.5	Hangtown	9	9	9	13	12
14	Williamson's	10	10			
16	Salsbury's	12	11	11	17	14
19	Alder Creek	14	13	12	19	16
22.5	Folsom	17	15	14	23	18
26.5	Carpenter's	20	17			
29	White Rock	22	18	17	30	25
34.5	Cothrins	26	20	19	35	26
38	Latrobe	26	15	14	28	26
43.5	Dugans	32	28	26	45	30
49	Shingle Springs	37	32	30	50	30

The railroad bridge completed in 1870 was a great accomplishment for the California Pacific. This detail is from Augustus Koch's *Bird's Eye View of Sacramento*, published in 1870.

Piles for the first bridge across the Sacramento, the Old Truss Bridge, were driven in 1857. It was also the first swing-span bridge in the state and served until 1870.

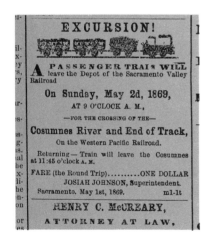

sake, but no relation to the present Western Pacific, was incorporated in 1862 to build 137½ miles of track from San Jose through Stockton to Sacramento. The job was completed after the C.P.R.R. took over when the Western tracks joined those of the Sacramento Valley Rail Road at Brighton Junction in 1870.

There were other construction problems to plague the Central Pacific Railroad but they were increasingly distant from Sacramento. In the city itself the railroad already was operating, hauling passengers and freight to Junction 16 months after construction began. The city thrived with railroad-generated commerce and the Big Four were no longer just local merchants. They had emerged as international financiers and political forces in the state and nation, even though Stanford was the only one actually to enter politics.

It is sufficient for this account to say that the Central Pacific did, indeed, join with the Union Pacific near some obscure desert rock called Promontory in Utah on May 10, 1869. The city exploded in celebration when it received telegraphed confirmation: "Done." The continent had been spanned.

Its major task done, the Central Pacific regrouped to fight off competition which had begun to develop in what it was inclined to claim as its "natural territory."

For example, a "war" erupted between the "CP" and a company known as the California Pacific—incorporated in 1865—when it laid track between Vallejo and Washington, in Yolo County across the River from Sacramento. "Cal-P" completed its roadbed in 1868 and extended its service to Marysville. It wished to enter Sacramento, and sought to do so, but the Central Pacific, with its extensive track and levee dockage, would not permit it.

It is said that even before the ground-breaking for the Central Pacific on Front Street in 1863, work had begun on the bridge across the American River.

Cal-P had bought boats and franchise from the California Steam Navigation Company and had been successful in controlling freight rates between Sacramento and San Francisco. Rebuked in its effort to enter Sacramento, the company formed the Yolo-Sacramento Bridge Company as a subsidiary to Cal-P, and spanned the river with a crossing capable of supporting trains. However, Cal-P had to cross tracks of the Central Pacific near the eastern end of the bridge, and Central Pacific was determined Cal-P would not do so. Violence flared. C.P.R.R. hands tore up Cal-P's newly laid track; but Cal-P rebuilt, and on January 29, 1870, made its first crossing over the Sacramento, with passengers.

Central Pacific resorted to the courts. Court commissioners ruled the new line must pay Central Pacific more than $360,000 for damages. But on appeal, the Supreme Court rescinded the order; it held it invalid. The rulings became academic the next year, however, when Milton S. Latham, a Cal-P director,

The 1870 bridge across the Sacramento appears at left in this artist's sketch.

sold his majority stock to the Central Pacific and the roads were merged, although Cal-P operated under its old name until 1876.

The Central Pacific would expand further. In 1869, the year it completed the line at Promontory, it bought out the California Steam Navigation Company which, with later purchases of such lines as the California Pacific, eventually gave Central a virtual transportation monopoly in northern California.

It was all created out of the dream and the persuasions of a young man named Theodore Judah who had the technical genius to make substance of his dream.

Pony Express
to Telegraph

It is difficult in this age of instant communications and instant history to imagine how isolated were such frontier communities as Sacramento in the building years, the 1840s and 1850s. It took almost six weeks, for example, for Sacramento to learn Congress had admitted California to the Union. In his biography of John Bidwell, Rockwell D. Hunt tells of Bidwell putting the confirming documents in the care of Elisha O. Crosby's daughter, Mary Helen, for passage to California. She is reported to have hidden them in her umbrella during the crossing of the Isthmus of Panama via the Chagres River and the umbrella still may be seen at Sutter's Fort. The historic message reached Sacramento the following day aboard the river steamer *New World*. In all, 40 days had elapsed from the time Congress admitted California, on September 9, 1850, before the word reached this far western outpost on October 19, 1850. Moreover, letters shipped the long way oftentimes would take four months for delivery depending on the time of passage.

Small wonder, then, that the pioneers turned their imagination to producing new and faster means of communication. In 1860, 21 years after Captain Sutter first debarked to begin the Sacramento settlement, one form of faster communication came through the introduction of the Pony Express. This romantic and dramatic episode in the early history was to survive only 1½ years, however, before it would be made obsolete, by progress toward transcontinental communication by telegraph.

But first the Pony Express. The idea is credited to Senator W. M. Gwin of San Francisco, who persuaded William Russell, in partnership with Alexander Majors and W. B. Waddell in a St. Joseph, Missouri freight service, that the creation of a pony express linking the established East with the burgeoning West not only would be an important service to the nation but that it might make money. Russell said he doubted it would pay but, excited by the concept, he committed Majors and Waddell to the idea. As it turned out, it did not pay, but the three made the history books with the adventure.

Stations were established 10 to 25 miles apart, depending on the difficulty of the terrain. Five hundred horses of sturdy flesh were rounded up. Eighty young riders, answering to the adventure, were enlisted. Ten days after the first relay rider was dispatched from St. Joseph, the last relay rider arrived in Sacramento—western terminus of the express with hitching racks in front of the old Hastings Building which still stands at 2nd and J. The date was April 13, 1860. The mail delivery was 80 letters. The messenger was met first at Sutter's Fort,

which by then had been reduced almost to an abandoned derelict, and he was escorted into town to the salute of artillery.

Riders rode in relays up to 75 miles, and in that distance might change horses three, four, even five times, depending on the terrain. He was allowed two minutes rest at each relay. Then, back into the saddle.

The Express was to be replaced in 18 months with the introduction of transcontinental telegraph between the East and the West in 1863. By then, telegraph had been in existence on a local and limited basis in California since 1853 when the first telegraph company to incorporate, the California State Telegraph Company, completed a line from San Francisco through San Jose, Stockton, Sacramento, and Marysville. The first message was sent out of Sacramento to Marysville October 19, 1853, and to San Francisco October 24, 1853. The rates for transmitting a message from Sacramento to San Francisco were $2 for the first 10 words and 75 cents for each additional five words.

In 1860, the California State Telegraph absorbed the Alta California Company, and by October, 1861, Sacramento was hooked into the East-West telegraph relays. Eventually California State Telegraph had absorbed most independent companies, and had moved to control most of the telegraph in the state.

Thus was Sacramento brought by relays into the age of comparative instant communication—ocean packet to Pony Express to telegraphy.

On land the country was bridged by rail, seaboard to seaboard. By wire, it now was spanned Atlantic to Pacific by telegraphy.

SACRAMENTO RIVER

Sacramento: Capital City

Chapter Nine

T HE POTENTIAL WAS THERE from the beginning, but only Captain Sutter beheld it. Even on that hot August day of his arrival in 1839 Sutter sensed this verdant plain with its full-flowing rivers mingling in gentle confluence one day would be the seat of empire for the rich new land. He was right. One day it would be designated capital of a new state and become a point of rendezvous for history. The burgeoning city which sprang up on the banks of the two rivers when gold was struck in the Sierra was to become more than a supply house for Argonauts and Mecca for the merchant and the banker. It would become the seat of government for a state whose destiny would be to emerge as the most densely populated in the Union of States.

In a real sense it might be said that in the beginning, the capital was an idea in search of a building. The capital, in short, sought a capitol, and like the king in search of a nail for the horseshoe, it was willing to give a kingdom for one.

But more on this later.

It would not be faithful to suggest Sacramento was the overwhelming choice from the beginning. It was not. Some of the legislators were certain that when gold petered out in the mountain diggings Sacramento would disappear from the earth. Others were concerned about the city's vulnerability to floodwaters. Then there was the fire which threatened to wipe out Sacramento in 1852.

And it is true, as well, that most of the businessmen in Sacramento who first set up shops and boarding houses and hotels and a theater, the Eagle, along the Embarcadero thought not in terms of empire or government destiny. They were businessmen intent on the new opportunity. Certainly many of them expected that once the boom burst they would move on—except for the few who shared a certain faith in the young city's future and who saw in the designation "capital city" a rich new opportunity in itself. They proceeded to work to secure it for Sacramento.

The capitol, shown here in a detail from Koch's lithograph, helped move the center of activity away from the Embarcadero.

The Sacramento of the 1870s was a mature city, as shown here in Augustus Koch's Bird's Eye View. *The transition from Sutter's Fort to Capital City was complete.*

The capitol at San Jose, 1849–1851

The Early Capitols

The City of San Jose was California's first capital, so designated by delegates to the Constitutional Convention held in 1849 in Monterey.

After voters overwhelmingly ratified the document on November 13, 1849, the newly elected lawmakers gathered for their first session the next month, December, in San Jose.

By pioneer standards San Jose even then was an "old" city. Its settlement predated statehood by almost three-quarters of a century. For in 1777, Lieutenant José Moraga, representing the Spanish government, had led 14 familes to the San Jose Country.

But for all of its established look, the influence in San Jose may have been too strongly Mexican to suit the new lawmakers; the memory of California's recent quarrels with Mexico, and the new allegiance to the Union, turned the pioneer lawmakers to seek new ground to plant root. Or as other accounts suggest, perhaps the dissatisfaction with San Jose stemmed from its lack of accommodations and its isolated location.

Seizing upon the opportunity, the gregarious Mariano Vallejo conjured up a new town on the northeastern shores of San Francisco Bay in the rolling country long associated with the family of the popular Mexican turned American. He came forward with a plan for a capital city which he intended to build from the ground up, and he would be its namesake.

Vallejo's proposal gained the approval of the cramped and discontented

186

The capitol at Monterey, 1849

lawmakers who grudgingly agreed to endure the deficiencies of San Jose until 1852 when they could move into their "New Capitol" in Vallejo.

Señor Vallejo went to work but time overtook him. On the fifth of January, 1852, the legislators who made up the state government journeyed to the new city of Vallejo, buoyed with optimism they now would have relief from the limitations of the San Jose site. Their smiles dissolved into groans, then to anger, over what they found. The affable Vallejo had tried his best; he had not had time to prepare for the legislature. The accomomdations he had erected were woefully inadequate.

Faced with the challenge of getting on with the business of the new state, the lawmakers threw up their hands in desperation that so seemingly simple a matter as quarters—a place to meet—should be their most pressing problem.

The capitol at Vallejo, 1852–1853

Sacramento Comes Forward

Enter Sacramento. The city was in the position, the enviable position, of being able to offer the waspish legislature a home. In 1850, in the spirit of doing everything big, the young city—then hardly established as a government itself —had chosen to build beyond its needs. It had constructed a courthouse of rather grand dimension, 50 feet by 75 feet, which boasted two stories. It had been completed only two weeks before the crisis faced the new state government at Vallejo—a capital with no capitol. Would the legislators like to hold the session in Sacramento?

The lawmakers accepted, eagerly. They boarded the steamer *Empire* and moved to the City of the Plain for the 1852 session.

The arrival did not go unattended by the young city. The legislators were greeted by parade and by handshake. A grand ball was arranged in the Orleans Hotel at $20 a ticket.

Sacramento still was not the capital, of course. It had the seat of government but San Jose still was capital, legally, and Vallejo still had dreams of completing his new capital city—from the ground up—and winning permanent designation.

In April 1852, Vallejo got his second chance. A bill was passed declaring the City of Vallejo to be the seat of government and ordering the governor to house all state records there. Sacramento, it appeared, would get its courthouse back.

In January 1853, the lawmakers found Vallejo was unable to complete his ambitious work, and that he was ill-prepared, as he had been ill-prepared the

The first courthouse in Sacramento County was completed in 1851. The existence of such a substantial structure is credited with bringing the capital to Sacramento.

A blackened hulk and scattered rubble was all that remained after the courthouse burned in July of 1854. Rebuilding started immediately.

previous year, to accept the legislature. So the legislature adjourned again—this time to Benicia where it found rather handsome, if small, quarters. The legislature made it clear it had no more patience with Vallejo.

Meantime Sacramento had had a taste of prestige in being host, if only briefly, to the legislature. The following year, 1854, with the legislature again meeting in Benicia, Mayor J. R. Hardenbergh and the Sacramento Council sent a communication via Governor Bigler, a Sacramentan, offering free use of the courthouse with its safes and vaults, as well as a deed to a block of land, free, bounded by I and J, 9th and 10th, as the site for a new capitol.

It was an attractive offer. State Senator A. P. Catlin of Sacramento introduced a bill to designate Sacramento permanently as capital city and stipulating that the state would accept the offer of the courthouse as temporary accommodations, and the block of land for a future capitol. The measure was passed. Sacramento had been designated capital city. The legislature's circuit ride in search for a permanent home   Monterey to San Jose, to Vallejo, to Sacramento, to Vallejo, to Benicia, and finally the return to Sacramento—was at an end.

Not even the fierce fire of 1854, which leveled seven-eighths of the city and which destroyed the new courthouse the legislature had occupied as capitol, discouraged those who were determined that Sacramento, come whatever, would remain host. Hardly had the flames died down before the county contracted to construct a new courthouse tailored especially to the needs of state government.

It was to be an impressive Ionic structure fronted by a portico supported by 10 massive pillars. It contained on its two floors chambers for both the senate and the assembly and for constitutional officers, including the treasurer and controller, with fireproof vaults. The building sprawled over an area 80 by 120 feet, and rose more than 60 feet. Perhaps most amazing of all, it was

The capitol at Benicia, 1853–1854

189

This even more impressive courthouse was finished in time for the 1855–56 legislature and provided more room for the function of government.

completed and occupied by the state on January 1, 1855, just a few days more than three months after the laying of the cornerstone.

There is another story told in history.

Justices of the California Supreme Court were reluctant to make the move to Sacramento. They gave legal persuasion to their refusal by ruling as unconstitutional the 1854 law designating Sacramento as capital city and held that San Jose remained the legal capital. Time took care of that objection. New justices were appointed; and since the legislature paid no heed to the court's admonition—that it was sitting illegally in Sacramento and should return to San Jose—the court finally followed the legislature to the new capital, taking offices in the Hastings Building at 2nd and J in 1855.

Sacramento had shown it wanted the capital. The legislature had made it clear it wished to sit in Sacramento. For the next 15 years the legislature met in the Sacramento courthouse, with the exception of 1862 when high waters again flooded the city; it met that year in San Francisco. Meantime, it planned for its new, permanent building—a home of its own: a Capitol.

As it has been said, the courthouse was the lure Sacramento used to attract

state government to Sacramento but it never was intended to be the permanent capitol. It offered no room for the Supreme Court. State agencies soon were forced to find office space in other buildings of the business district. The legislature was aware of the necessity and by April 18, 1856, the two houses passed a bill to issue $300,000 worth of bonds to build a state capitol on the lot given to the state in the city's original proposal.

The building was to rise in the block—bounded by I and J, 9th and 10th—on one of the squares deeded to the city by John Sutter, Jr. for public plazas. The legislation called for the structure to be completed by 1858.

Competition was intense among architects who sought the distinction of designing a monument to the 31st state. The board of capitol commissioners, set up to administer the construction, chose the plans of Reuben Clark and let the contract to Joseph Nougues, the contractor who built the courthouse the legislature had been occupying as capitol since 1855.

The first shovel of dirt was turned in December of 1856. The project which would have changed the face of the city had begun. But the times were not prosperous. The blush was off the bloom of the Gold Rush and the state was in considerable debt. The city saw in the construction of the capitol a harbinger for better times.

Within two weeks after groundbreaking, work on the capitol came to an abrupt halt, however. State officials refused to release the necessary money for the work on the ground that the bonds were "unconstitutional" and the state could not afford so immense an expenditure in a time of economic stress. The contractor Nougues disagreed. He took the matter to court but he failed in his suit to force construction. Almost as quickly as it began, work at the J Street site ceased—never to resume. And it was not long before the state returned the block to the city which subsequently turned it into a city plaza, landscaped and known to this day simply as The Plaza.

Agitation continued for construction of a capitol the state could call its own but nothing was done for another four years, until 1860, when the County of Sacramento—anxious to reclaim its courthouse for its own use—deeded to the state

A Capitol

The state rejected the plan shown here for the capitol. The architect is unknown, but he was one of many competing for the $1,500 prize for the best design.

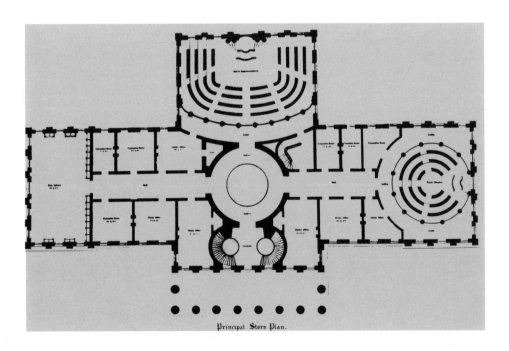

Principal Story Plan.

the major portion of four large and attractive blocks—L to N, 10th to 12th. The state still was obliged to buy the remainder from 50 different owners for $16.368.33.

Prodded, the legislature turned again to the old issue of raising its own capitol and appropriated $500,000 to build the new structure on the new site. The City Council quickly accommodated the plan by moving to close streets and alleys; by September of 1860, all buildings in the blocks had been condemned and had been sold at auction. The ground was prepared for construction.

Again architects competed for the right to design the new capitol. This time M. F. Butler won the state's approval, and he earned, as a prize, $1,500 for submitting the best plan. With the prize went something more practical and more generous: appointment as superintendent of construction.

As an aside, there were those who felt Reuben Clark should have won the award. They pointed out that Butler's plan was astonishingly similar to the plan offered by Clark years earlier for construction on the downtown Plaza site. Clark was to be stricken with mental illness and to enter the asylum for the mentally ill in Stockton, early in 1866.

The cornerstone was laid May 15, 1861, at the northeast corner of the building; finally construction was under way. The undertaking was to be tested once more, however. In 1862 a devastating flood, perhaps the largest flood crest to inundate the city, reached the construction site, leaving the foundations weakened. The capitol commissioners called a halt at once to construction to determine the full extent of the damage. Considering the ever-present danger of new floods, they decided on a solution: they would raise the foundation walls another six feet lest floods strike again. The result was that the cornerstone became buried even further and now rests well below the ground level.

Nor was construction of so massive a structure in the time of Civil War easy. The legislature was nervous about advancing funds to keep construction going. Materials were increasingly in short supply, especially those on order from the Eastern seaboard. Still the work went on—maddeningly slow, perhaps, but it went on.

The specifications called for a capitol made of California granite to symbolize the sturdy stuff of which the new state was made. Again, supply and transportation—and money—became increasingly frustrating factors, and so the plan was reviewed. And even before completion of the first floor it was decided to proceed with the rest of the construction in brick. So brick, not granite, it is.

In a publication, the state office of architecture and construction recreated the building years thus, in part:

Foundation trenching for the northern portion of the building was followed by laying of cobblestones in the trench. Over this base, three layers of concrete were poured, each layer of which was one foot in thickness. The concrete consisted of "gravel the size of pigeon's and hen's eggs mixed with Hoffman's Rosendale cement from New York."

Brickwork began in the middle of February 1861. By May of 1861, the brick

The bills below were submitted by suppliers for materials used in the new capitol.

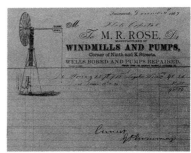

A capitol made of sturdy California granite appealed to the legislators and the people, but after the first floor was completed cost and other problems dictated a change to brick. The view at the top left looks to the northwest. The two pictures at lower left show the dome rising, and below is the building as it looked in early 1869. By then it had the appearance of a state house but the scaffolds and ladders are still in place.

walls of the northern portion had been completed to a height of about five feet above the surrounding ground level. On May 15, 1861, the cornerstone was laid at the northeast corner of the building just below the newly established ground level. Extensive flooding that year, however, resulted in a decision to raise the walls six feet higher than originally planned, thus placing the cornerstone still further underground.

The construction proceeded slowly over the ensuing years due to the problems of funding and of delivery of materials. During the period of the Civil War, many construction items which might have been ordered from the East were, instead, made in San Francisco where facilities for such manufacturing were limited.

After completion of the roof in 1868, it was possible to look forward to occupying the partially completed building. In November, 1869, Governor Haight and the Secretary of State moved into their new quarters. In December, 1869, the Legislature held its first session in the new chambers. At this time of occupancy, much of the exterior work was still not completed including the entrance porches, steps and porticos, the rotunda above the apex of the roof, the dome structure, balustrades, certain granite work, exterior doors and trim, the entire third floor and the interior plumbing work.

The capitol began to rise above the surrounding skyline long before it was completed, and while many pointed to it with pride, such reaction was not universal. A visitor, perhaps a little vexed that the prestigious structure was not located in his particular region, wrote an amusing but somewhat degrading description of the entire Sacramento scene in the July, 1870 *Overland Monthly* magazine. Disguising his identity behind the unlikely *nom de plume* of Socrates Hyacinth, the writer actually was Stephen Powers, who became a respected ethnologist and studied California Indians in later years. His general comments were biting and lengthy, but his irreverence toward the Capitol must serve as a sample:

Among the buildings, one naturally goes first to visit the Capitol. In approaching it, one's eye, of course, falls first upon the little dome, which, with its flag-staff, looks like an aggravated case of a wart, or a sort of mole, with a hair growing out of the top of it. But it would be cruelly unjust to judge the Capitol in its unfinished condition. (Do I not rejoice in that reason for not being obliged to pass an opinion?)

Meantime, the State Supreme Court, which had been so reluctant to move with the legislature to Sacramento, heard its first case in the chambers designed for it in December, 1869, in the capitol. As a matter of fact, the court beat the legislature in occupying the capitol by days.

Much still remained to be done but Sacramento had waited long enough. So on the fifteenth of December, 1869, a grand ball was organized with all the pomp the city could bring to it. There was dancing in the chambers of both the senate and the assembly; a burdened board offered supper in the hall. It was a magnificent affair. With the construction, 15 years of transient lodging in two courthouses and the conduct of state business from rented offices scattered throughout the downtown city ended. With the construction, California at long last could point to its own symbol of commonwealth, the capitol. And it rose splendidly on the plain.

The final jewel in the construction—the crown jewel, it might be said—

was not installed until October 30, 1871, however, when a gold ball—it remains today—was put in its place high atop the cupola on the dome. Weighing perhaps 60 pounds and made from a copper core plated with gold smelted from $300 in coin, the sphere was placed on a wooden stand which rests today in the State Archives and was signed by workmen and dignitaries who braved the altitude for the occasion. The exact height of this golden globe has been variously reported from 212 to 230 feet. M. S. Westervelt put it at 219 feet 11½ inches above the level of 10th and Capital Avenue. Dr. J. N. Bowman, a state archivist, reported in 1960 that he calculated it at 225 feet 10-11/16 inches above the ground.

The cost for the Capitol to this point was reported to be $1,939,585.84.

When the work was declared fully completed on February 8, 1874, the cost was said to be $2,600,000. Hardly a large figure by today's estimates, but a staggering sum in its day.

The capitol stood handsome and ready by 1869 as workmen put on the finishing touches. At year's end the legislators moved in and the gold sphere was placed on top.

From Fort to Capital

With the occupation of the capitol, exactly 30 years had passed since John Sutter brought civilization to the inland frontier and birth to a city which would be called the City of the Plain.

The fort, in the year 1869, was an abandoned relic, shelter for vagrants and playground for youth. The clapboard and the canvas which rose on Front had disappeared long ago. No longer did miners tramp through this portal to the gold fields, or wet their thirst at the play pens of the Old City. Now the city was established. It had survived several major floods and two great fires; it had been designated capital of a state whose name already had become synonymous with adventure, and had become legend.

It is said that a city is never finished, and of course it is not. With each new sculpting hand, the sculpture changes.

But still, if one looks hard enough, he reads the telltale story of the city's old life in the fragments left behind. And he lives anew the adventure of a time past, and of people past. The beginning had come to an end.

Bibliography

Reading list of some materials which were helpful in developing background for the preparation of this work:

Barber, Edmund Lorenzo and George Holbrook Baker. *Sacramento Illustrated.* (Sacramento: Barber and Baker, authors and publishers, 1855). Reprinted in 1955 by Sacramento Book Collectors Club.

Benton, J. A. *The California Pilgrim: A Series of Lectures.* (Sacramento: Solomon Alter, 1853)

Burnett, Peter H. *Recollections and Opinions of an Old Pioneer.* (New York: D. Appleton & Co., 1880)

Colville, Samuel, compiler and publisher. *Samuel Colville's City Directory of Sacramento for the year* ——. (Colville published several directories, beginning in 1853–54 when he included Dr. John F. Morse's first history of the city. All are valuable sources.)

Dana, Julian. *Sutter of California.* (New York: The Press of the Pioneers, Inc., 1939)

Davis, Winfield J. *An Illustrated History of Sacramento with General Chapters by W. J. Davis.* (Chicago: Lewis Publishing Company, 1890)

Duflot de Mofras. *Exploration du Territoire de L'Oregon des Californies.* (Paris: Libraire de la Societe de Geographie, 1844). 2 volumes.

Gay, Theresa. *James Marshall, the Discoverer of California Gold, a Biography.* (Georgetown, California: The Talisman Press, 1967)

Grimshaw, William Robinson. *Grimshaw's Narrative, being the story of life and events in California during flush times.* Written for Bancroft Library in 1872. (Sacramento: Sacramento Book Collectors Club, 1964)

Gudde, Erwin G. *Sutter's Own Story.* (New York: G. P. Putnam's Sons, 1936)

Guinn, Professor J. M. *History of the State of California and Biographical Record of the Sacramento Valley.* (Chicago: Chapman Publishing Company, 1906)

Kemble, Edward. *A History of California Newspapers.* Reprinted from the supplement to the *Sacramento Union,* December 25, 1858, edited with a foreword by Helen Harding Bretnor. (Los Gatos: The Talisman Press, 1962)

Kotzebue, Otto von. *A New Voyage Round The World In The Years 1823, 24, 25, and 26.* In two volumes. (London: Henry Colburn and Richard Bentley, 1830)

Lagomarsino, Barbara. *Early Attempts To Save The Site Of Sacramento By Raising Its Business District.* (Masters Thesis: California State University, Sacramento, 1969)

Letts, J. M. *California Illustrated.* George V. Cooper, illustrator. (New York: R. T. Young, 1852)

Massett, Stephen. *Drifting About, An Autobiography.* (New York: Carleton, 1863)

Meyer, Carl. *Bound for Sacramento,* translated by Ruth Frey Axe. (Claremont, California: Saunders Studio Press, 1938)

Reed, G. Walter. *History of Sacramento County, California.* (Los Angeles: Historic Record Company, 1923)

Simpkinson, Francis Guillemard and Captain Edward Belcher. *HMS Sulphur at California, 1837 and 1839.* Edited by Richard A. Pierce and John H. Winslow. (San Francisco: The Book Club of California, 1969)

Stillman, J. B. D. *The Gold Rush Letters of J. B. D. Stillman,* with an introduction by Kenneth Johnson. (Palo Alto: Lewis Osborne, 1967)

———. *Seeking the Golden Fleece.* (San Francisco: A. Roman and Company, 1877)

Sutter, John A. *New Helvetia Diary.* (San Francisco: The Grabhorn Press, 1939)

Taylor, Bayard. *Eldorado.* (New York: G. P. Putnam, 1850) 2 volumes.

Taylor, William. *California Life.* (New York: Carlton and Porter, for the author, 1858)

Thompson, Thomas H. and Albert Augustus West, publishers. *History of Sacramento County, California.* (Oakland, California: Thompson and West, 1880)

Willis, William L. *History of Sacramento County, California.* (Los Angeles: Historic Record Company, 1913)

In addition to the works cited, many more were consulted. No attempt was made to tabulate the numerous newspapers consulted in the research. These may be found at the California State Library, the Bancroft Library at the University of California, the California Historical Society, and other depositories.

Picture Credits

Bancroft Library: Pp. 60–61, 68, 102 top. California Historical Society: Pp. 14–15, 52 bottom, 64, 65, 72, 138, 149, 157. California State Archives: Pp. 25 top, 28, 192, 193. California State Library: Pp. 9, 26 left top and bottom, 29, 31, 32, 34, 35, 35 top, 37, 38 top and bottom, 39, 43 bottom, 44, 45, 55, 56 top, 59, 71, 74, 78, 79, 92, 95, 105, 109, 116, 121 top left, and lower right, 123 middle, 128, 131, 132 bottom, 143 top right and bottom right, 150 top and bottom, 151 top and bottom, 152, 153, 154–155, 156, 160, 162–163, 168 bottom, 170 top, 171, 172–173, 174, 175 bottom, 176 left and bottom, 179 top, 180 top, 182, 183, 186, 187 top and bottom, 189 bottom, 194 bottom left and right. Collection of Herb Caplan: P. 194 top. Crocker Art Gallery: P. 136. M. H. de Young Museum: P. 161. Collection of Michael Harrison: P. 17. Huntington Library: Pp. 40, 107 top, 144 top. Hutchings Magazine: P. 198. Oakland Museum: Pp. 10, 101, 177 top. Collection of Roger Olmsted: P. 112. Sacramento *Bee* Printing Museum: Pp. 11, 12–13, 16, 19, 20, 22 top and bottom, 23, 24, 25 top, 26–27, 36 bottom, 41 top and bottom, 46, 47, 48, 49, 50, 51 bottom, 52 top, 53 top and bottom, 54, 56 bottom, 57, 58 top and bottom, 60, 62, 63, 66, 67, 69, 75, 76, 77, 88, 89, 90–91, 93, 94, 96–97, 98–99, 100, 102 bottom, 103 top and bottom, 106, 107 bottom, 108, 111, 114, 118, 120 top and bottom, 121 top right and lower left, 122, 123, top and bottom, 124, 127, 132 top, 133 bottom left, 134, 139, 140, 141 bottom, 142 top, 143 left, 145 left and top right, 146, 147, 158–159, 166 top and bottom, 167, 168 top, 169, 170 bottom, 175 top, 178 top and bottom, 179 bottom, 180 bottom, 181 bottom, 184, 185, 188, 189 top, 190, 191. Sacramento City-County Library: Pp. 181 top, 195. Sacramento City-County Museum: Pp. 56 bottom, 113, 135, 165, 177 bottom, 197. Society of California Pioneers: Pp. 43 top, 51 top, 164. Southwest Museum: Pp. 70–71.

CAPTAIN JOHN A. SUTTER.

Capt. Sutter was born in Switzerland, near the close of the last century, but passed most of his youthful days in France, where his gallant conduct obtained for him an honorable commission. After the wars of the continent were over, he emigrated to the United States, and served several years on the Western frontier, principally in Missouri, from whence he turned his steps to the Pacific, and arrived in Oregon in the fall of 1838, from whence he soon after sailed in the bark Clementine, for the Sandwich Islands. He came to San Francisco from the latter place in the month of July, 1839, and proceeded to Monterey to obtain permission from the government to locate in the Territory.— Capt. Sutter engaged the schr. Isabella, a pinnace and a launch, and was eight days engaged in exploring the Bay in order to find the mouth of the Sacramento River. He then proceeded to the mouth of Feather river, and returned to the American river, landing at the site of what is now called the Old Tan Yard, in the month of August. He then selected a place of residence at the point where Sutter's Fort has since been erected.— One year afterwards he was appointed to the office of Military Commandant of the North. The Exploring Expedition came here in 1841. About six years after Captain Sutter moved to Hock Farm, where he has since resided. His wife, daughter and younger son, who had continued in Europe, after many years' separation, rejoined Captain Sutter in 1850. What fortune soever may be in store for this distinguished man, he will ever have a strong hold upon the respect and love of his fellow countrymen.

SUTT

MARYSVILLE.

Marysville was laid out on the Yuba, one mile above its junction with Feather river, in the fall of 1849, and has already attained a position of fourth or fifth in size and population among the cities of California. That the citizens are of a highly enterprising and progressive character, is shown by their determination and success in overcoming the difficulties to which the place is subjected from the low stage of Feather and Yuba rivers during the dry season. This year by a liberal appropriation for the purpose of removing snags from the streams, most of the impediments and dangers of navigation have been overcome. The trade of Marysville is very large, being the depot of supplies for the entire Feather river gold region and several extensive districts on the Yuba, furnishing supplies for the